Revolutionary Lives

Series Editors: Brian Doherty, Keele University; Sarah Irving, University of Edinburgh; and Professor Paul Le Blanc, La Roche College, Pittsburgh

Revolutionary Lives is a book series of short introductory critical biographies of radical political figures. The books are sympathetic but not sycophantic, and the intention is to present a balanced and where necessary critical evaluation of the individual's place in their political field, putting their actions and achievements in context and exploring issues raised by their lives, such as the use or rejection of violence, nationalism, or gender in political activism. While individuals are the subject of the books, their personal lives are dealt with lightly except in so far as they mesh with political issues. The focus of these books is the contribution their subjects have made to history, an examination of how far they achieved their aims in improving the lives of the oppressed and exploited, and how they can continue to be an inspiration for many today.

Published titles:

Leila Khaled: Icon of Palestinian Liberation
Sarah Irving

Jean Paul Marat: Tribune of the French Revolution
Clifford D. Conner

www.revolutionarylives.co.uk

Gerrard Winstanley

The Digger's Life and Legacy

John Gurney

First published 2013 by Pluto Press
345 Archway Road, London N6 5AA

www.plutobooks.com

British Library Cataloguing in Publication Data
A catalogue record for this book is available from the British Library

ISBN   978 0 7453 3184 3   Hardback
ISBN   978 0 7453 3183 6   Paperback
ISBN   978 1 8496 4676 5   PDF eBook
ISBN   978 1 8496 4678 9   Kindle eBook
ISBN   978 1 8496 4677 2   EPUB eBook

Library of Congress Cataloging in Publication Data applied for

This book is printed on paper suitable for recycling and made from fully
managed and sustained forest sources. Logging, pulping and manufacturing
processes are expected to conform to the environmental standards of the
country of origin.

10   9   8   7   6   5   4   3   2   1

Designed and produced for Pluto Press by Chase Publishing Services Ltd
Typeset from disk by Stanford DTP Services, Northampton, England

To Rachel, Thomas and Anna

Contents

Acknowledgements

My thanks to Ann Hughes for suggesting that I write this book, and to David Castle and Brian Doherty for all their expert advice and help. In the course of working on the book I have had valuable exchanges on Winstanley with Scott Ashley, Fabrice Bensimon, Andrew Bradstock, Jeremy Boulton, Ian Bullock, Fergus Campbell, Colin Davis, Martyn Hammersley, Rachel Hammersley, Ariel Hessayon, Geoff Horn, Ann Hughes, William Lamont, David Taylor and Derek Winstanley, and I am grateful to them all. Rachel, Thomas and Anna have been immensely supportive and patient throughout – this book is dedicated to them, with love.

1
Introduction

In the summer of 1918, as the first anniversary of the October Revolution approached, steps were taken in Moscow to implement one of Lenin's pet projects, his plan for monumental propaganda. According to a decree that had been issued on 12 April, surviving symbols of the Tsarist regime were to be systematically removed, and monuments to past revolutionary thinkers and activists set up along major routes in the metropolis. Similar plans were laid for Petrograd. Among the old Tsarist symbols which faced destruction was a large granite obelisk standing prominently in the Alexander Gardens by the Kremlin, and which had been erected as recently as 1913 to commemorate 300 years of Romanov rule. It was Lenin who took the decision to save the obelisk, when it became clear that re-use might be preferable to demolition. As civil war in Russia intensified, work on new monuments had proved much more difficult than expected, and it was apparent that few would be ready for the first anniversary celebrations. It made good sense to recycle an older monument, even at the risk of upsetting Moscow's avant-garde artists and sculptors. The Romanov two-headed eagle was removed from the Alexander Gardens obelisk, and the names of tsars were effaced; in their place the names of 19 leading revolutionary thinkers were inscribed. As might be expected, Karl Marx and Friedrich Engels headed the list, but the eighth name was that of 'Uinstenli', or Gerrard Winstanley (1609–76), best known as leader of the seventeenth-century English Diggers, who in April 1649 had occupied waste land at St George's Hill in Surrey, sowed the ground with parsnips, carrots and beans, and declared their hope that the Earth would soon become 'a common treasury for all, without respect of persons'.[1]

The Alexander Gardens obelisk, Moscow. Winstanley is eighth on the list, after Marx, Engels and other leading revolutionary thinkers. Credit: Mitrius (wikimedia commons).

Why should Lenin and his associates have chosen Winstanley as one of the thinkers whose work might be seen to have helped pave the way for the massive upheavals of October 1917? What was it that brought Winstanley into this Pantheon of great revolutionaries, and provided a link, however tenuous, between the English and Russian revolutions? At first sight, the presence of Winstanley's name seems puzzling. Winstanley was not particularly well known even in his own time, and he was certainly not one of the dominant figures of his age. His period of public activity lasted for only a brief, four-year period from 1648 to 1652, and the Diggers were active for little more than a year before their colonies in Surrey and elsewhere were broken up, their crops trampled and their houses burned. In the two centuries after Winstanley's death his writings were read by only a small number of people, and it was not until the last decade of the nineteenth century that his life and works became better known, and socialists came to rediscover a figure who appeared to anticipate many of their own beliefs. The mid-century Chartists had known and praised the Leveller leader John Lilburne, but Winstanley passed them by.[2] His rediscovery came too late even for Marx and Engels, to whom Winstanley's ideas were apparently completely unknown.[3] There is no evidence that William Morris, the English socialist whose *News from Nowhere* might seem to indicate a knowledge of Winstanley's writings, had ever read a word of them. It was Eduard Bernstein who in 1895 provided the first systematic analysis of Winstanley's ideas in his contribution to Karl Kautsky's *Forerunners of Modern Socialism*, thus enabling Marxist intellectuals for the first time to appreciate their significance.[4]

Winstanley was a religious thinker and visionary, strongly influenced by the mystical writings that were so popular among radicals in the English Revolution; his work was suffused with biblical quotation and he shared fully in the millenarian excitement of the age. In many ways there was a world of difference between him and late nineteenth-century Marxists. Yet it is possible to understand how the latter might come to take an interest in Winstanley and to see in him a precursor, however distant, of Marx. Winstanley's views were always distinctive: he chose to use the word Reason in place of the word God, he insisted that humanity and the whole creation had been corrupted by covetousness, competitiveness and false dealings, and he anticipated a time when all would come to recognise the virtue of abandoning private property and working in common. In Winstanley's writings Marxists could find some of the most trenchant criticisms of contemporary social relations to appear from a seventeenth-century pen, and they would readily have acknowledged the importance of his insight that only a wholesale transformation of society, brought about by knowledgeable, regenerate individuals working together, would rid humankind of suffering and exploitation.[5] All of society's and the earth's problems could, it seemed, be linked to the rise of private property and monetary exchange; the creation of a moneyless and property-less society was not only desirable but inevitable. The forthcoming transformation – the 'restoration of all things' – would be liberating for all, rich as well as poor.[6] To late nineteenth-century students of Marx, Winstanley's vision of 'community' might appear consistent with their understanding of communism – a word first coined in their own century. Through a close reading of Winstanley, they might also – as Eduard Bernstein and Georgi Plekhanov both did – spot rudimentary attempts to formulate familiar Marxian concepts such as alienation and the labour theory of value.[7] It is no wonder that Bernstein, who did so much to make Winstanley's writings better known, could in 1895 describe Winstanley as being well ahead of his contemporaries, and praise the skill with which he made connections between the social conditions of his time and their causes.[8]

Winstanley's appeal to Marxists lay not only in his perceptive social criticism, but also in his recognition of the importance of agency and self-emancipation. Like many seventeenth-century radicals Winstanley proclaimed his preference for action over words, but while some radicals advocated charitable help for the poor, Winstanley was insistent that the poor should take responsibility for freeing themselves from their burdens. The actions of the poor in working the land in common, and in refusing to work for hire, would both signal the impending changes and help usher them in. Marxist readers of Winstanley, deeply engaged as many of them were in the political struggles of their own time, would find no difficulty in endorsing Winstanley's observation that 'action is the life of all, and if thou dost not act, thou dost nothing'.[9]

In his religious writings too Winstanley might be seen to have gone further than many of his contemporaries. His deep anti-clericalism was directed not only against the institutions and personnel of the established church, but against all organised religion, including the radical sects. Marxists encountering Winstanley for the first time would welcome Winstanley's fierce criticism of the social functions of religion, and of versions of Christianity that focused primarily on individual salvation. It was actions here on earth, rather than any promise of future salvation, that for Winstanley formed the essence of true religion; the question of the existence of heaven or hell was consequently of lesser concern to him. While most historians today would identify Winstanley's religious position as an extreme example of a belief in a religion of conduct, it is easy to understand why turn-of-the-century Marxists might see him – as many of his contemporaries had – as at heart an atheist, and as someone who used religious language principally to cloak secular arguments. In this, as in so many other ways, Winstanley could appear to them to be one of the most interesting forerunners of modern scientific socialism.

The true picture is, of course, more complex. Even in the first few years after Winstanley's popular rediscovery, his appeal seems to have been as great for anarchists and libertarians as for orthodox Marxists. As early as 1899, the radical journalist and land campaigner Morrison Davidson was able to describe Winstanley as 'our seventeenth-century Tolstoy', and he was only the first of many to seek to associate the Digger with an anarchist rather than Marxist tradition.[10] The struggle for Winstanley between Marxists and anarchists continued for much of the twentieth century. While in the late 1940s Communist Party intellectuals championed Winstanley as a materialist and a supporter of state action, George Woodcock could claim him in 1944 as a thinker who anticipated Kropotkin's idea of Mutual Aid 'as he anticipated anarchism in so many other ways'.[11] George Orwell too believed that Winstanley's thought 'links up with anarchism rather than socialism'.[12]

Academics too soon came to see him as a figure of particular significance. The rise of modern academic interest in Winstanley is often associated, quite justifiably, with the work of the Oxford historian and Marxist Christopher Hill (1912–2003), whose contribution to our understanding of the Digger phenomenon remains highly influential. But many other professional historians, of a wide variety of political opinions, have added over the years to our knowledge of Winstanley's life and ideas, as have leading literary scholars, theologians, legal historians and political scientists. Voices of dissent are occasionally still heard, and the attention devoted by scholars to Diggers and other civil war radicals is still sometimes characterised as 'wildly disproportionate'.[13] Such comments may seem rather quaint and old fashioned today, a throwback to the 1950s when it was still possible to study mid seventeenth-century British history at degree level without hearing any mention of Winstanley's name.[14] But it is clear that in academic circles interest in Winstanley has never been the sole preserve of the left. The great Victorian historians S.R. Gardiner and C.H. Firth both took notice of Winstanley's writings, while Perez Zagorin, certainly no Marxist, could in the 1950s praise Winstanley as a 'genius' and 'one of the pre-eminent political thinkers of his time'. Even the redoubtable G.M. Trevelyan felt able to declare that Winstanley was of the 'most attractive and noble type ever produced by our island', and a figure well worth rescuing from the obscurity into which past prejudice had scandalously cast him.[15]

Winstanley became a writer and activist in the late 1640s, in the aftermath of England's civil wars, and he can only properly be understood in the context of the political, economic and religious crisis of the post-war years.[16] The period from 1640 to 1660 – which encompassed civil war between king and parliament, the defeat and execution of Charles I, and the experiments in kingless rule that followed – is most commonly referred to today as the English Revolution.[17] It was Christopher Hill who promoted the view that these two decades witnessed England's most significant period of bourgeois revolution, and much of the focus of his early work was on the nature and dynamics of that revolution.[18] From an early date, however, he also acknowledged the existence of an unfulfilled radical revolution that could be set alongside the one that succeeded, and it was here that Winstanley was seen to belong.[19] By the time Hill came to write his ground-breaking book *The World Turned Upside Down*, which was published in 1972, his interests had turned firmly to this 'revolt within the revolution'.[20] Among the multitude of radical figures discussed in the book, Winstanley clearly stood out as the real hero, and the true revolutionary.

The World Turned Upside Down was re-issued in paperback in 1975, and this helped to ensure that Winstanley's ideas, set in the context of the radical ferment of the revolutionary decades, reached a much wider readership than ever before. Winstanley's own work had also become available for the first time in a relatively cheap and accessible form, in Hill's 1973 Pelican Classics edition of Winstanley's *The Law of Freedom and Other Writings*.[21] Both books had a widespread influence, and it is partly to them that we can ascribe the exceptional fame that Winstanley has come to enjoy. The singer-songwriter Leon Rosselson recalled being 'fired up by discovering Winstanley' in *The World Turned Upside Down*; after reading it he sought out other books on Winstanley and wrote his Digger song 'The World Turned Upside Down: Part 2', which has since become one of the best-known protest anthems of recent years.[22] Hill's books were also read widely by students at the new British universities established in the 1960s – where radical ideas featured prominently in the many English Revolution 'special subjects' set up by admirers or former students of Hill – and at Oxford, where his influence remained strong even after his retirement. At Sussex, which quickly established itself as a leading centre of English Revolution studies, two special subject students in the 1970s reputedly followed Winstanley's example and went off to set up their own commune.[23]

It was outside academia that Hill's books had their most direct impact, and where interest in Winstanley has since grown most quickly. In recent decades Winstanley has become one of the most widely-celebrated figures from the period of the English Revolution, today perhaps more famous even than the Leveller leaders. There have been plays, TV dramas, novels, songs and, in

Kevin Brownlow and Andrew Mollo's *Winstanley*, an important film. Politicians of the left have often cited him as an inspirational figure.[24] His ideas and achievements have come to be seen as being particularly relevant to modern activists, and the Diggers are one of the historical groups with which activists today are most likely to identify. From the 1960s Haight-Ashbury Diggers, through Britain's Hyde Park Diggers and Digger Action Movement, to twenty-first-century land campaigners, G20 Meltdown protestors and Occupy movement activists, there have been frequent echoes of Winstanley's writings in the activities of modern social movements.[25]

Who then was Winstanley? What were the influences on his ideas, and what brought him to lead the occupation of the Surrey commons and to risk – and persuade others to risk – the violence, cold and hardship that awaited the Diggers on St George's Hill? What became of Winstanley after the end of the digging, and how should we assess his posthumous reputation and the steady growth of interest in him over the past hundred years? What is it today that gives Winstanley's ideas such an important place in radical popular memory? It is the aim of this book to address these questions, and to provide an account of Winstanley's life and writings. But in order to understand the making of the Digger we need to explore the road that took him to St George's Hill.

2

The Making of the Digger

On a wet morning in September 2011, a small group of marchers passed through the town of Wigan to Mesnes Field, a popular open space threatened with development. Armed with spades, and dressed variously in broad-brimmed hats and specially commissioned T-shirts, members of the crowd posed for local photographers before symbolically planting their spades in the turf and starting to dig. Later that day they were joined by others in the Old Pear Tree pub in Fig Lane, to hear speeches and talks on Gerrard Winstanley, to drink and to listen to bands and choirs including the Bolton Clarion Choir singing the Digger anthem 'You Noble Diggers All'.[1] All those present were there to celebrate Wigan's first Diggers' Festival and to remember Winstanley, who was born in the town and baptised in All Saints Church on 10 October 1609. The festival banner proclaimed the Diggers to be 'England's and the World's first pioneer socialist and political movement of the common people'; it was adorned with the extracts from Winstanley's writings most favoured and quoted by modern activists:

For freedom is the man that will turn the world upside downe; therefore no wonder he hath enemies...

Words and writings were all nothing, and must die, for action is the life of all, and if thou dost not act, thou dost nothing.[2]

The festival aimed to raise public awareness of Winstanley in the town of his birth, a town which had often celebrated its links to figures such as George Formby, Georgie Fame and Sir Ian McKellan, but which had made little of its connections to the Digger leader. Even among those who regularly visited Gerrard Winstanley House, home to the town's Unison branch, Citizens

Advice Bureau and MPs' constituency offices, few, it seemed, had much awareness of the meaning or significance of the building's name.[3] The festival organisers hoped that, given time, a regular Diggers' Festival might 'attract crowds comparable with the annual Durham Miners' Gala and Tolpuddle Martyrs' Festival', and that justice would thereby be done to the memory of Winstanley and his followers.[4]

Gerrard Winstanley was born in Wigan just over 400 years before the town's first Diggers' Festival took place. He belonged to an ancient local family, and was the son of Edmund Winstanley, a Wigan mercer.[5] His mother may have been the Jane Doman of Wigan who married an Edmund Winstanley on 27 January 1601, but we cannot be sure.[6] Wigan was a large and populous parish, and the town, which lay at its heart, was one of Lancashire's most prosperous.[7] Four main streets, Wallgate, Hallgate, Standishgate and Millgate, radiated from the Market-place, moot hall and parish church, and in these streets could be found the houses and business premises of the town's leading inhabitants. A great many of Wigan's male inhabitants were burgesses, and enjoyed voting rights and economic privileges denied to outsiders and other residents of the town.[8] Most burgesses lived within the confines of the town, but there were also quite substantial numbers of others, including local gentry, yeomen and successful former Wigan inhabitants who enjoyed rights as 'out burgesses'.[9]

Wigan's administrative structures were complex, and conflict was never far from the surface. The town's mayor, aldermen and burgesses jealously defended their privileges, not only from the demands of non-burgesses but also from the lord of the manor who was, unusually, also the rector of the parish. In the late sixteenth and seventeenth centuries relations between lords and tenants in Wigan were often difficult, and Winstanley will have grown up aware of the ill feeling that existed. Successive rectors sought to lay claim to their supposed rights as lords of the manor, and their claims were more often than not resisted by the townspeople, many of whom had come to believe that custom and practice had, over the years, given them *de facto* control over the manor.[10] Edward Fleetwood, rector from 1571 until 1604, and Dr John Bridgeman, who became rector in 1616, were particularly vigorous in asserting their rights.[11] As Ann Hughes has noted, Bridgeman's activities 'would not have given Winstanley a favourable impression of the established church', and may even have 'prompted his later association between rapacious landlordism and oppressive clerical power'.[12] One of the few rectors to choose to live more peaceably with his manorial tenants and to avoid outright confrontation was Dr Gerard Massie, rector and lord of the manor from 1604 until 1616. A noticeable rise in numbers of boys christened Gerrard or Garrard in the years 1608–13, including Gerrard Winstanley, may well reflect his standing among the more well-to-do parishioners of Wigan.[13]

Winstanley's father was a Wigan burgess, and he is known to have played his part in town affairs and to have participated in parliamentary elections. He served as churchwarden for the town in the plague year of 1625, and in 1634 he was one of three Wigan inhabitants to whom the lands of the town's grammar school were placed in trust.[14] He was one of 74 Wigan burgesses who voted in the elections for the 1628 parliament, but his name is absent from the lists of votes for the Short Parliament of 1640.[15] It seems likely that he was the Edmund Winstanley of Wallgate who died in 1639 and was buried in December of that year.[16]

We cannot be certain about Winstanley's religious background. Wigan, like other Lancashire parishes, was deeply divided along religious lines. A good many inhabitants and neighbouring gentry, including a number of Winstanleys, had kept to the old faith at the Reformation, while others had been vigorous supporters of the break with Rome.[17] In 1605, just four years before Winstanley was born, an Edmund Winstanley and his wife were among those presented for attending unlawful religious meetings in the town of Wigan.[18] It is not known whether these were Winstanley's parents. If Gerrard's father was a churchwarden in Wigan in the 1620s, it seems unlikely that he would have flirted with separatism, though the possibility remains open. Winstanley's own testimony suggests that in his youth he was a regular and uncomplaining churchgoer.

What we can be certain about is the close involvement of
Winstanley's immediate family in the cloth trade, which was
of increasing significance to Wigan in the early years of the
seventeenth century. The town was well known as a centre of
woollen and linen manufacture, drawing both on local supplies
and, increasingly, imports of linen flax from Ireland. Many of
its inhabitants were also becoming involved with new branches
of manufacture, especially cotton.[19] Much of the finished cloth
found its way to London, where Wigan-born citizens were
active as merchants or as factors operating from Blackwell Hall,
London's main textile mart and an important destination for
Lancashire cloth.[20] Winstanley's father was, as we have seen,
a mercer, one of only a small number operating in a town in
which most trades were tightly controlled by the corporation
and court leet.[21]

The importance of London as the chief market for Lancashire
wool, linens and cottons ensured that increasing numbers of
Wigan-born individuals entered the cloth trade in the capital.
They worked as haberdashers, merchant taylors and drapers,
and helped foster trade links between Lancashire and London,
sometimes as independent merchants and sometimes as partners
or factors in more extensive family enterprises. Some very
complex family, kinship and business networks developed, with
successful London merchants maintaining close links with their
home town and establishing contacts with other Wigan-born
Londoners active in the legal profession or church. A number
of those who came to London made substantial fortunes,
and several left money for Wigan's poor, the town's grammar
school or other local causes when they died.[22] Some quite
distant relatives were also able to benefit from their links to
these successful London inhabitants, either through bequests of
money or through offers of employment.[23] Winstanley was one
beneficiary of family contacts with Wigan-born Londoners. On
19 April 1630, when he was 20 years old, he was apprenticed
to Sarah Gater, who ran a cloth business in the London parish
of St Michael Cornhill.[24] She was the widow of William Gater, a
London clergyman turned merchant taylor who had previously
served as lecturer to Henry Mason, a native of Wigan and rector

of St Andrew Undershaft. The Mason and Gater families were related, and William Gater's first apprentice had been Mason's nephew. It is possible that Winstanley was another relative.[25]

Winstanley worked with Sarah Gater until at least February 1638, when he became free of the Merchant Taylors' company and set about establishing his own cloth business.[26] As the historian James Alsop has shown, Gater's household was a religious one and she possessed a well-stocked library. She remained on good terms with her relative Henry Mason, who gave her several of his books, and she was sufficiently close to her 'dear cousin' the well-known author Izaak Walton to name him as an overseer of her will.[27] We can only speculate about the intellectual influence that Gater and her circle had on Winstanley. Mason was a prebendary of St Paul's Cathedral and former chaplain to Bishop King of London. He was the author of popular devotional works and a friend of leading London divines, and he had an important part to play in the City's religious community in the 1620s and 1630s.[28] He fashioned a plain and direct style in his published works, a style that finds distinct echoes in Winstanley's writings. Although there is nothing very profound about Mason's devotional tracts, one can occasionally see glimpses in them of the sorts of psychological insight that were to be so characteristic of Winstanley, and it would be surprising if the future Digger did not encounter these works while he lived in Gater's household.[29]

Winstanley was later to recall that he had once been a 'blind Professour' and 'strict goer to Church, as they call it, and a hearer of Sermons', who 'never questioned what they spake, but believed as the learned Clergy (the Church) believed'. It is possible that it was when he was living in Gater's household that he began to gain this reputation, and came to be 'counted by some of the Priests, a good Christian, and a godly man'.[30] If Mason was one of those who came to wield an influence, however slight, over Winstanley, that influence may have been a troubling one for the young apprentice. In the early years of the seventeenth century the Church of England had been broadly Calvinist in doctrine, but this consensus was undermined by the rise of Arminianism, a movement whose adherents rejected Calvinist beliefs in absolute reprobation – or the eternal damnation of the mass of humankind. In later decades, and in other hands, a rejection of the rigidity of Calvinist doctrine would often be associated with religious radicalism, but this was not how Arminianism was seen in the 1620s and 1630s. The Arminian movement gained ground with the accession to the throne of Charles I in 1625, and with the appointment of William Laud as Bishop of London in 1628 and Archbishop of Canterbury in 1633.[31] Laud's version of Arminianism combined deep hostility towards Calvinist doctrine with a vigorous promotion of the role of the clergy and of ceremonial in church worship, and many saw it as coming dangerously close to Catholicism. In the 1620s Mason had been regarded as a conciliatory figure who mixed easily with both Calvinists and anti-Calvinists, but by the mid 1630s he had become much more closely linked to the Laudian camp.[32] He had always sought to portray himself very much as a loyal and grateful son of the Church of England, 'the purest and best reformed Church in Europe', and had vigorously defended the church in print against Rome, but he came increasingly to align himself with Laudian reforms in the church and to be seen as an opponent of Puritanism.[33] In 1641 he would be forced to leave London when parliament moved decisively to rid the church of all traces of Arminian innovations.

In his devotional writings Mason showed respect for the poor and distaste for the pursuit of material wealth, but this was combined with strikingly confident arguments in support of conventional church teachings on inequalities of wealth and power.[34] Those who lacked wealth or authority had, Mason declared, no 'right to that; which they so greedily desire', for 'all things are God's, and he may dispose them at his pleasure'; we 'should rather give thankes for what we have, than grudge for that which wee want'. Our duty is to accept that 'that State is best for us, which God doth allot unto us', and to esteem those gifts which God in his wisdom has given others more fortunate than ourselves.[35] In this, as in much else, Mason's views appear wholly at odds with the beliefs that Winstanley would come to espouse. Mason was, however, not the only Arminian with whom Winstanley came into contact: many of the clergy he would have encountered in his first few years in London were, like Mason, on the conservative wing of the church. While Winstanley lived and worked in Gater's household it is likely, as Alsop has pointed out, that he worshiped regularly in the parish church of St Michael Cornhill where the minister was William Brough, another clergyman associated with the Arminian cause.[36] Brough was chaplain to the king, and like Mason he would be driven from his living in the 1640s. When Winstanley set up independently in business, he settled in the City parish of St Olave Old Jewry. The minister there was Thomas Tuke, yet another Arminian and future royalist, and another who would lose his living during the Civil War.[37]

The first certain record we have of Winstanley as an independent householder comes from May 1639, when he was due to pay parochial assessments in St Olave's from the previous Christmas. He took on his only known apprentice, Christopher Dicus, the son of an Essex minister, in June.[38] It was in September 1640, while he was still busy building up his business, that he married the 27-year-old Susan King.[39] She came from a medical family: her mother, who was also named Susan, was a midwife, her father, William King, was a prominent surgeon, and two of her sisters had married surgeons earlier the same year. William King was a member of the Barber Surgeons' Company, and was appointed senior warden in 1646 and master of the company in 1650.[40] At the time of Winstanley's marriage to Susan, King was in possession of a reversion to one of the four surgeons' places at both St Bartholomew's and St Thomas's Hospitals, the latter reversion having been gained with the personal support of Sir John Bramston, Chief Justice of the King's Bench.[41] King was eventually appointed surgeon at St Bartholomew's in October 1643, following the death of John Woodall, the well-known author of *The Surgeon's Mate*.[42] The King family were resident in London, but at some point in the 1630s or early 1640s, in a development that would be of crucial importance for Winstanley and the history of the Digger movement, they also acquired a small estate in the parish of Cobham in Surrey, worth between £30 and £40 a year.[43] This estate was probably intended only for occasional occupation, but it was later to become the permanent home of Susan and Gerrard Winstanley and the place from which the Digger experiment would be launched.

Winstanley's move to Cobham came after the collapse of his business, a process that was hastened by the onset of civil war. In 1640, when Charles I's eleven-year experiment in rule without parliament came to an end, Winstanley's modest enterprise was still relatively new, and it stood little chance of surviving the crises that would engulf the nation. The king had been forced by financial pressures, brought on by rebellion in Scotland and the war that followed, to revert to calling a parliament. The 'Short Parliament', which assembled in April 1640, was quickly dissolved, but the parliament that met in November proved more resilient. MPs were determined to reverse recent innovations in church and state, and to set their institution on a more secure footing. Londoners were soon caught up in the religious disputes, demonstrations and petitioning and fundraising campaigns that became such a marked feature of public life in 1641 and 1642, and popular participation in the kingdom's affairs reached unprecedented levels: Winstanley's parish church of St Olave's was just one of several in which religious riots took place.[44] The outbreak of rebellion in Ireland in November 1641 drove king and parliament further apart, and in January 1642, following his failed attempt to arrest his leading opponents at Westminster, the king was forced to flee London. Over the next few months further divisions opened up in the political nation, as increasing numbers of MPs and members of the gentry became alarmed at the high levels of disorder in town and countryside, and anxious about the rapid pace of religious reform being pursued by more zealous parliamentarians. Both king and parliament began raising forces, and by 22 August Charles had sufficient support to be able to raise his standard at Nottingham. This was the moment when England's Civil War officially began.

The events of these years affected Winstanley's business directly. The Irish rebellion disrupted trade with Dublin: Philip Peake, a Dublin merchant with whom Winstanley had traded, became indebted to him for the substantial sum of £114, and this sum was still unpaid eleven years later.[45] Matthew Backhouse, a Barbados merchant, soon owed him £150.[46] From late 1641

Winstanley's payments to fellow merchants became less frequent than before. He made no payments to Richard Aldworth, one of his major creditors, between the end of November 1641 and 6 May the following year, and the last of his regular payments to Aldworth came on 29 October 1642.[47] By then civil war had broken out, the first great battle had been fought at Edgehill, and the king's forces were preparing for their advance on London. The disruption of war, and the heavy demands of the parliamentarian war effort, proved too much for the young merchant. In the autumn of 1643 Winstanley abandoned his trade, vacated his house and shop and left London for Surrey. He made a final payment to Aldworth on 30 November, and by 20 December he and Susan were settled in Cobham.[48] His own later account of the move to Cobham is brief, but shows clearly where he felt the blame lay for the collapse of his business:

> By the cheating sons in the theeving art of buying and selling, and by the burdens of, and for the Souldiery in the beginning of the war, I was beaten out both of estate and trade, and forced to accept of the good will of friends crediting of me, to live a Countrey-life.[49]

His views on the trading activities in which so many of the City's inhabitants were engaged, and in which he had been heavily involved, became unreservedly hostile. As he was to remark in *Truth Lifting up its Head Above Scandals* (1648), 'Men that are guided by principles of fair dealing void of deceit, know not this day how to live, but they will be cheated and cosoned'.[50] He was more explicit still in *The New Law of Righteousnes* (1649), when he declared:

> For matter of buying and selling, the earth stinks with such unrighteousnesse, that for my part, though I as bred a tradesman, yet it is so hard a thing to pick out a poor living, that a man shall sooner be cheated of his bread, then get bread by trading among men, if by plain dealing he put trust in any.

Trading had, he added, 'generally become the neat art of thieving and oppressing fellow-creatures, and so laies burdens, upon the Creation'.[51] We should be wary of assuming too simple a causal link between the collapse of Winstanley's business and his subsequent radicalisation, but the experience clearly had a profound effect on the way he viewed the world; certainly he was to draw heavily on it when he came to justify his heterodox religious ideas and his programme for revolutionary change.

Elm Farm (formerly Emmetts), Cobham. Emmetts, the adjoining Smiths or Smythes, and Mill Field (now Cobham Cemetery), were farmed by Winstanley from the 1640s to the 1670s. Credit: John Gurney.

The move to Cobham represented a major reverse for Winstanley. Having spent several years learning his trade and assiduously building up his business, he was now forced to give up his home and his trade. He also found himself resident of a rural parish in Surrey, a very different type of community from London or the Wigan of his youth. Cobham was situated in mid Surrey, lying between the towns of Kingston and Guildford and at some distance from each. To the north was the river Thames and the populous village of Walton-on-Thames, and to the north west the large expanse of St George's Hill, which formed part of the extensive commons and waste of the manors of Walton and Walton Leigh.[52] Cobham also contained large tracts of common and waste. One of the biggest was the Tilt, and it was near here, along the road leading from Church Cobham to Stoke d'Abernon, and close by the River Mole, that Gerrard and Susan Winstanley eventually settled.[53] Today the sites of their properties are occupied by modern farmsteads and Cobham Cemetery, but there is no plaque to record their presence there. Winstanley's connection with the parish has, however, not been wholly forgotten. A visitor to Cobham can walk the Heritage Lottery funded Diggers' trail, seek out the mosaic image of Winstanley in Cobham's pedestrian precinct, or see the new housing in Winstanley Walk and Winstanley Close. Winstanley is also remembered in the parish church, where a plaque was unveiled in September 2009 to commemorate the 400th anniversary of his birth. Andrew Whittle's Diggers' Memorial Stone, which was carved in 1999 for the 350th anniversary of the Digger occupation of St George's Hill, has found a permanent home near Weybridge Station after permission to erect it on the hill was refused.[54]

It was long thought that Winstanley was reduced to near destitution after his move from London, and that in Cobham he was forced to take work as a labourer herding cattle. From what we can gather from his writings, however, it is evident that he was responsible for running the holding he occupied and was involved in grazing or dairying.[55] We do not know whether he lived independently at first, or was always a tenant or agent of his parents-in-law. What we can be certain of is that Winstanley was a householder who derived an income from farming and was liable for paying taxes and other local charges; he was also liable to attend Cobham's annual view of frankpledge or court leet.[56] The old view that he became a hired labourer can no longer be sustained, and it was in fact after his move to the parish that he first came to style himself 'gentleman'.[57]

This is not to suggest that Winstanley's life in Cobham was easy. The county of Surrey was spared the most serious fighting of the Civil War, but its inhabitants did not escape the violence completely; they also faced many financial exactions, both in

terms of formal assessments and of free quarter (or the quartering
of soldiers in exchange for a promise – rarely honoured – of
later payment).[58] Civil war taxation in Cobham was unusually
heavy, and the parish, which was crossed by the main London
to Portsmouth road, was also subject to the frequent passage of
troops. Cobham's inhabitants complained in 1645 that the 'great
burden' of free quarter had 'caused some of the parish to forsake
there habitations not being able to continue'.[59] Winstanley was
one parishioner who would later claim that 'by the burthen of
Taxes and much Free-quarter, my weak back found the burthen
heavier then I could bear'.[60]

The parish of Cobham was also troubled by long-standing
social tensions, of which Winstanley would quickly have become
aware. A marked rise in population in the decades before 1640
had contributed to a sharpening of social differences in the
parish, as the numbers of poorer inhabitants rose significantly
and the position in society of husbandmen or small farmers
declined.[61] For many years there also had been conflict between
landlords and manorial tenants, deriving principally from the
serious financial problems experienced by the Gavell family, the
lords of the manor of Cobham. In struggling to fend off their
creditors and predatory neighbours, the Gavells had resorted
to challenging manorial customs that protected their tenants'
rights and interests at the expense of their own. In the late
sixteenth and early seventeenth centuries they and their tenants
had engaged in a lengthy series of suits in the courts of requests
and chancery, and in the succeeding decades they did their best
to maintain a tight control on manorial administration.[62] There
was nothing particularly unusual about Cobham's tradition of
landlord-tenant conflict, for similar conflicts could be found in
numerous parishes and manors across southern England. But
Winstanley evidently took note of the inequalities and patterns
of exploitation he witnessed in his adopted parish, and they will
have had a profound influence over the development of his ideas.

Landlord–tenant conflict was exacerbated by the war,
in Cobham as elsewhere.[63] Unusually, Cobham's manorial
administration survived the Civil War with only minimal
disruption, and presentments against tenants and others

who infringed the customs of the manor were still regularly brought. Among those presented before the manorial court was Winstanley, who was one of six Cobham inhabitants fined in April 1646 for digging peat on the common.[64] By this time the manor of Cobham had a new lord, John Platt. Platt was an ordained minister and had recently been appointed rector of West Horsley in Surrey. He had married Margaret Gavell, the daughter of Sir Humphrey Lynde, a well-known religious controversialist who had settled in Cobham in his old age; Platt now held the manor in right of his wife and her son.[65] For the first time since his youth in Wigan, Winstanley found himself living in a parish where the lord of the manor was also a minister, and Platt's determined attempts to uphold the rights of Cobham's manorial lords may well have brought back memories of the unhappy relations between Wigan's townspeople and Bishop Bridgeman. In his writings Winstanley would target both the clergy and lords of the manors, and it is no doubt significant that in two important periods in his life the roles of minister and lord of the manor were merged into one.

Winstanley certainly learnt much from his short time in Cobham, for one of the most telling aspects of the Digger programme was its successful fusion of religious with social radicalism and its skilful appropriation of traditional languages of rural discontent.[66] Winstanley drew frequently on local experience when providing examples of the gentry's failings towards the poor, as when he complained of their exploitation of the commons and accused them of interfering whenever the poor 'cut Wood, Heath, Turf, or Furseys, in places about the Common, where you disallow'.[67] His Cobham experiences must also have provided the basis for the quite subtle analysis of contemporary rural social relations he displayed in his Digger writings – one that differentiated the poor not only from the gentry but also from 'rich Freeholders', those prosperous yeomen who joined with the gentry in making 'the most profit of the Commons, by your over-stocking of them with Sheep and Cattle' while the poor were left with the smallest share.[68] He wrote this while the Diggers were on St George's Hill, but the issue of access to the commons continued to rankle when he wrote his last work, *The Law of Freedom*. In this he again complained that the 'rich Norman Free-holders, or new (more covetous) Gentry, over-stock the Commons with Sheep and Cattle; so that inferior Tenants and poor Laborers can hardly keep a Cow, but half starve her'. The poor, he concluded, 'are kept poor still'.[69]

It is clear that throughout the civil war years Winstanley was a vigorous supporter of parliament. In 1642 he had sided with reformers in a franchise dispute in St Olaves, and by his own account he contributed financially to the parliamentarian cause at the start of the war.[70] He willingly took the Solemn League and Covenant[71] on 8 October 1643 while still in London, and after his move to Cobham he was present when, in February 1644, members of the Surrey clergy and of the parliamentarian county committee took the covenant in Kingston-upon-Thames.[72] We also know that he continued to maintain contacts with London, and made frequent visits to the capital. In 1644 he informed against Robert Holt, a London merchant taylor of his acquaintance whom he suspected of lying about his contributions to the parliamentarian cause. This incident shows him becoming identified increasingly with parliament's more militant supporters, and demonstrates his willingness to risk the loss of old friendships for the sake of the greater cause. His actions in this case may be seen as typical of those who portrayed themselves as the Saints – those godly individuals who set themselves apart from the mass of humankind and who were prepared to subordinate all else to the pursuit of God's cause.[73] Winstanley's denunciation of Holt almost certainly came at the time that he was undergoing the profound religious experience that led him to abandon his old religious outlook and to seek a wholly new spiritual path. We cannot know for certain the precise religious path that he followed in the 1640s, but we can tentatively see him as moving from orthodox Protestant to Baptist, Seeker and finally Digger.

The 1640s were years of religious flux and innovation. During the Civil War the Church of England was effectively dismantled, moves were taken to abolish episcopacy and, in 1645, William Laud, the Archbishop of Canterbury, was executed on Tower Hill.[74] Civil war divisions were as much religious as political, with royalists fighting to preserve what was left of the old church and established forms of worship. On parliament's side, religious divisions were exacerbated by the entry into England's Civil War of the Scots, who sought as the price of their participation a Presbyterian church settlement in England, a settlement that would be wholly unacceptable to religious Independents in parliament and the army. The smooth running of parishes was disrupted as many ministers were driven out for suspected royalism or 'obnoxious' beliefs, and as others moved to more lucrative livings made vacant by expulsions – Cobham was one parish that lacked a regular minister after 1643. The breakdown of traditional hierarchies and authority, and the consequent freeing up of the press, allowed for the expression of new ideas, and the wide circulation of heterodox ideas that had previously been accessible only to a minority. The emphasis for many was on fluidity and experimentation, and on experimental learning rather than book learning: the spirit was as much a guide as the scriptures.[75] The teachings of the university-educated clergy could be disregarded, as could all forms of worship which stood between the individual and God. As heresiographers like the London clergyman Thomas Edwards noted, sectaries who set themselves up as teachers were free to spread their 'errors' in many parts of the country, converting others who might themselves then develop their own unique brand of ideas. Given the instability of religious forms and doctrines in the 1640s it is perhaps unnecessary to look too closely for distinct influences. Older heretical ideas that had survived relatively unchanged in the religious underground of the late sixteenth and early seventeenth centuries could take on wholly new forms when exposed to new audiences during the Civil War. Readers of the many writings from the spiritualist tradition which became easily accessible for the first time through cheap publications might take on board some arguments but discard others, in ways the authors and their immediate followers would never have intended; ideas were constantly being refashioned and reworked in original and unexpected ways.

As is the case with so many other radical thinkers from the time of the English Revolution, it is almost impossible to identify which works or individuals had the greatest immediate impact on Winstanley. The emphasis on experimental knowledge and on the workings of the spirit meant that no intellectual debts were ever likely to be acknowledged: as Winstanley himself put it, 'I have nothing, but what I do receive from a free discovery within, therefore I write it, to set forth the spirits honour, and to cast a word of comfort into a broken and empty heart.'[76] The problem for scholars was expressed bluntly but effectively by David Petegorsky in 1940, when he suggested that 'to search for the sources of [Winstanley's] theological conceptions would be as futile as to attempt to identify the streams that have contributed to the bucket of water one has drawn from the sea'.[77] Apart from the Bible and John Foxe's *Acts and Monuments* – a work familiar to almost all literate English men and women of the seventeenth century – there is very little that we can say for certain about Winstanley's reading.[78] Some have suspected that Winstanley knew, and was influenced by, the ideas of the German mystic Jacob Boehme, but Ariel Hessayon's recent research suggests that no discernible influence can be found. We should perhaps, as Hessayon points out, pay more attention to the originality in Winstanley's thought than to attempts to trace his intellectual lineage.[79]

We have seen that Winstanley had had contacts with anti-Calvinist ministers when he was first in London. There is also evidence that for a time he moved in Calvinist, Presbyterian circles.[80] At some unspecified point in the 1640s Winstanley went, as he later put it, 'through the ordinance of dipping'.[81] We know little about this Baptist phase, or how long it lasted. The Baptists were the first of the great radical religious movements of the 1640s, their influence spreading in the army and far beyond London. The movement had two distinct wings, the Particular Baptists – who retained a belief in Calvinist notions of election and reprobation (some would be saved but most were eternally damned) – and the General Baptists, many of whom combined a belief in particular election with a rejection of eternal reprobation.[82] Ariel Hessayon has recently suggested that the radical Winstanley emerged from within a General Baptist milieu, and he has drawn attention to similarities between some of Winstanley's most characteristic ideas and significant General Baptist tenets.[83] The argument is persuasive, but we still cannot be sure how closely involved Winstanley ever was with the General Baptists.

In Winstanley's early writings we find distinct echoes too of figures like Thomas Collier, who was much closer to the Calvinist Particular Baptists – though in the 1640s he differed from them on a number of significant issues. Collier was described by Thomas Edwards as a 'master sectary', and he was one of those who travelled across southern and western England gathering converts, and who developed an efficient network of followers and emissaries.[84] He is known to have spent time in Surrey, as did the General Baptist preacher Thomas Lambe, and it is possible that Winstanley made contact with him on one of his preaching tours. Collier's vigorous anticlericalism comes through clearly in his surviving writings and sermons from the 1640s, as does his decidedly Winstanley-like hostility to 'carnall' notions of heaven as a 'glorious place above the Firmament, out of sight, and not to be enjoyed till after this life'. For Collier, like Winstanley, God should not be seen as being 'afar off', for where 'God is manifesting himselfe, there is his and the Saints kingdome, and that is in the Saints'. The second coming was spiritual rather than literal, 'an internall and spirituall change, a transformation out of the nature of the first into the nature of the second Adam'. Christ's 'glorious Kingdome in the Spirits of his people', and the power it gives to the Saints were, for Collier, 'the new heavens and the new earth'.[85] Much of this sounds very much like the early Winstanley – and like a number of the other religious radicals who came to prominence towards the end of the 1640s. Phrases and concepts that were to take on particular importance in Winstanley's Digger writings appear frequently in Collier's published works from the later 1640s.[86] We need not assume that Winstanley was ever a follower of Collier, and indeed the differences between them, particularly in relation to salvation, might be said to outweigh the similarities. It is however hard to believe that Winstanley never read Collier or heard him preach, or that Collier was wholly unfamiliar with Winstanley's writings. The points of similarity between them also serve to remind us how much Winstanley's own, highly distinctive religious views clearly drew on many of the ideas and concepts that were being circulated and openly discussed by religious radicals in the 1640s. The question of whether he picked some of them up from Collier is perhaps of less importance than the question of how exactly he made use of them.

If Winstanley ever truly identified with the Baptists, he was soon to distance himself from them, and they from him. In the period leading up to his first publication, Winstanley's religious views were probably closest to those of the Seekers – individuals who rejected ordinances, withdrew from all existing churches and sought instead to wait on the Lord in private, 'pretending to no certain determination of things, nor any infallible consequences or interpretations of Scriptures'; and who waited 'for a restauration of all things'.[87] The Seekers, though important in the later 1640s, are by their very nature among the most difficult religious groups to study, and we should be cautious about assuming that Winstanley was ever actually one of them.[88] But there are many obvious similarities between Winstanley and the Seekers, not least in his rejection of outward forms and emphasis on the 'free discovery within', and in his insistence that he never presumed to teach others. Like the Seekers, Winstanley had also become as critical of gathered congregations, with their tendency to restrict membership to a few, as he was of the established church. Separation was, he would later argue, 'no more but going out of one form into another, not into the unitie of the one Spirit'. All outward forms were to be shunned, and 'those that worship Christ at a distance in their severall Congregations and forms, and are most zealous therein, are in these dayes the most bitterest enemies to the ministration of Christ in Spirit and in truth'. Winstanley was, he maintained, always willing to 'break bread with any in whom I see but the least measure of the Father rising up' and to 'suffer others to walk to that measure of knowledge they have received, though it differ from mine'.[89]

Winstanley's earliest publications appeared in quick succession in the spring and summer of 1648. Although not all of them bore a publisher's or printer's name, it is likely that they were all issued by Giles Calvert, the London bookseller who had had already gained a reputation for publishing the works of many of the most significant radical thinkers.[90] Winstanley's early writings have often been portrayed as dense and impenetrable, and showing few signs of things to come. George H. Sabine, the editor of the major 1941 edition of Winstanley's works, provided only brief abstracts of the three earliest publications. Petegorsky saw the first two as 'typical of the chiliastic mysticism so popular during the period', a mysticism which he believed Winstanley quickly abandoned as his argument became more 'that of a progressive rationalist'. There was, Petegorsky felt, 'little in them to indicate the trend of Winstanley's later development'.[91] More recently scholars have come to pay much greater attention to the early writings and to acknowledge their importance for any study of the development of Winstanley's ideas. Although the communism of his later works could barely be discerned in these writings, a number of important aspects of what we find in his mature programme were already becoming apparent.

The first two publications, *The Mysterie of God* and *Breaking of the Day of God*, were overtly millenarian works, and strikingly anti-clerical and anti-formalist. They expressed Winstanley's optimistic belief in universal redemption – and the ultimate salvation of all – a belief that was always to be of key importance for him and one that formed the essential basis for his later, more radical programme. It was a belief that set him apart from many of his contemporaries, and it was a dangerous one to hold in 1648 when parliament was working to strengthen the blasphemy laws to suppress heterodox beliefs of this kind. In all his early writings the essential goodness of humankind was emphasised, as was the need for each individual to abide by the Golden Rule – to do unto others as we would be done by. This concept had become a commonplace in radical discourse in the late 1640s, and was expressed by a wide variety of thinkers, but for Winstanley it was to be of particular significance and central to his philosophy.[92]

In his early works Winstanley took concepts familiar from the writings of others and reworked them to suit his own, very particular arguments. To Thomas Collier, for instance, 'the New

Creation, the Kingdom of Heaven in the Saints', was 'the great Mysterie God is now revealing to them'.[93] Winstanley accepted that the light would rise first in the Saints, but in his conception of the mystery of God he rejected the narrow focus that Collier and others like him placed on a small body of the elect. For Winstanley the mystery of God lay in the redemption of *all*: 'every particular branch, Man and Woman' would be delivered from bondage, for God would 'dwell in the whole Creation, that is, every man and woman without exception'.[94]

In *The Saints Paradice* and *Truth Lifting Up its Head* we see the appearance of Winstanley's highly distinctive equation of God or the Spirit with Reason. Like Collier, Winstanley was critical of those who hold 'forth God and Christ to be at a distance from men', or think that 'God is in the Heavens above the skyes'. No one should 'imagine and fancie a God to be in some particular place of glory, beyond the skies, or some where he knows not, or in some particular place of glory that cannot be knowne till the body be laid in the dust'; he was, rather, 'the spirit within you'.[95] But Winstanley was not content to rest there. For him, the very name of God created difficulties, so he chose instead to talk of Reason, 'for though men esteem this word Reason to be too mean a name to set forth the Father by, yet it is the highest name that can be given him'. Reason was the great creator and 'governs the whole Creation', and if all were subject to the spirit of Reason within, then they would abide by the Golden Rule and cease to act unrighteously towards others. 'For the Spirit Reason', he argued, 'doth not preserve one creature and destroy another ... but it hath a regard to the whole creation; and knits every creature together into onenesse; making every creature to be an upholder of his fellow; and so every one is an assistant to preserve the whole.'[96] This was of course too much for some: Collier, for instance, was soon attacking the 'false light' that 'presents God to the understanding to be but a piece of reason, and so, that there is indeed no God, but reason rules al things, and upholds al things; questioning, if not denying the naming of God'.[97] But Winstanley's substitution of the name Reason for God illustrates well his shift towards an extreme religion of conduct – one that emphasised the central importance of conduct

towards others, and relation of the individual to the whole, as
the essence of true religion – and it necessarily prefigured the
development of his vision of a world in which all was restored
to perfection and freed from conflict, poverty and oppression.

We can also see early signs of Winstanley's developing
preoccupations in the use he made of the concept of the two
Adams, a concept that John Saltmarsh, Thomas Collier and other
radical thinkers had incorporated into their writings. Collier
believed that the supersession of the 'earthy' first Adam by the
heavenly, second Adam was very much an internal process, but
the benefits would be limited to the elect, for clearly 'all are not
saved with an eternall salvation'.[98] Winstanley, developing the
concept in his own distinctive fashion, adapted it to fit with
his belief in the salvation of all and with his growing sense of
the corruption brought about by self-interest. The 'lineage or
generation' of the first Adam was 'every particular branch of
man-kind, living upon the objects of the creation, and rejecting
their maker'; those who 'live upon the objects of the creation,
and not upon the spirit in the Creation' were 'but branches of
the first man'. The second Adam, 'a meek spirit, drawn up to
live in the light and strength of pure Reason', was destined to
triumph in each individual: 'and so the whole bulk of mankind,
when they shall be drawn up to live in the unity of the one spirit,
is the second man, and every son and daughter of this spirit,
is the lineage of this second man'. He would 'raign King of
righteousnesse in flesh, and spread as far in restoring all things,
as the first man corrupted all things'.[99] It would not take much
for Winstanley to move from this position to his conviction –
which was to inform all his Digger writings – that covetousness,
manifested in private property and buying and selling, lay at the
heart of all that was wrong with the world and was destined to
be replaced by the spirit of community.

By late 1648, Winstanley was a well-published writer who had
in a short time fashioned a distinctive message that enabled him
to stand apart from other, better-known preachers and authors.
No doubt this was a deliberate strategy, for in the crowded world
of 1640s religious radicalism it was always important to find
one's own voice, and to assert one's originality, while building on

ideas and concepts familiar from the work of others. No direct reference to these other authors was needed, for readers could be expected to know who they were. In each case Winstanley took ideas associated with others active at the time – the two Adams is but one example – and developed them in ways that were uniquely his. We can see this too in his emphasis on universal redemption, and in his very deliberate attempt to appeal to those who, like him, had become dissatisfied with all existing sects and churches. We can also see it in his respectful, though cautious attitude towards magistracy, and in the ways he was beginning to make use of – and radically rework – quite familiar aspects of parliamentarian propaganda to suit his arguments.[100] Although there was still some way to go before his ideas were fully developed and a clear sense given of his future direction, his was already a unique voice that compelled attention.

Winstanley did not set his early writings aside after he had the vision that led him to St George's Hill. In December 1649, at the height of the digging experiment, Giles Calvert reissued Winstanley's first five publications, both in separate editions and bound together as *Several Pieces Gathered into one Volume*. We should not dismiss this simply as a publisher's attempt to cash in on Winstanley's new-found fame, for Winstanley took the trouble to supply the introduction to *Several Pieces*, and it seems likely that he was responsible for a number of careful textual and typographical amendments found in the revised editions of his tracts.[101] Winstanley clearly did not see this early work as ephemeral, and of little relevance to the activities he was engaged in in December 1649. The five works were to be read together, and they stood alongside his Digger writings as definitive statements of his religious ideas. It is also significant that it was around the time of republication that Winstanley was working on two of his most significant religious tracts, *A New-Yeers Gift* and the communistic *Fire in the Bush*, works that were designed partly to remind readers of the essential theological foundations of the Digger programme.

Winstanley's early works were written against a background of unfolding political crisis. Parliament's military victory over the king had not brought political stability, and conflict between political 'Independents' and political 'Presbyterians'[102] in parliament, and between parliament and its army, helped keep royalist hopes alive and set the scene for the emergence of the radical, London-based Leveller movement.[103] Following the invasion of Parliament by Presbyterian apprentices in July 1647, and the consequent flight of many MPs and peers, the army had marched on London, and large numbers of troops were once more quartered in counties around the capital; free quarter again became a major grievance. In May 1648, Surrey joined other counties in petitioning parliament for a personal treaty with the king, government by known laws, and the disbanding of the army. Surrey's petition, which was brought to Westminster by thousands of supporters, including a number from the Cobham area, demanded nothing less than the restoration of the king 'to his due honour and just rights, according to our oaths of supremacy and allegiance ... from which no power on earth can absolve us'. Arguments between petitioners and soldiers guarding parliament quickly turned to violence, and by the end of the day up to eight petitioners were dead and many more assaulted and stripped. Shock at the soldiers' violent response was followed by anger, as Surrey's inhabitants declared their intention of defending themselves against outsiders and the army, and the backlash left committed supporters of parliament and religious radicals dangerously isolated from their more conservative neighbours.[104] Winstanley wrote of the 'cloud of nationall troubles' and the 'great bitternesse, envy, reproachfull languages, in and among men and women in these days, against others whom they brand Sectaries'. The people he now identified with most closely, and sought to reach out to in his writings, were those who were, he claimed, branded 'deceivers and troublers': those 'that they would plunder', who would be 'sentenced to be put to death in these uproar risings under the name of Round-heads', and who 'are counted the troublers of Kingdoms and Parishes where you dwell'.[105] The involvement of some Surrey inhabitants, including near neighbours of Winstanley, in the armed royalist rising which took place in Surrey in July could only have increased the sense of isolation for Winstanley and others like him.[106]

We know something about the circles Winstanley was moving in towards the end of 1648. One of his acquaintances at this time was a Kingston separatist, John Fielder, who had become involved in a bitter dispute with Kingston's minister, bailiffs and constables. Fielder had begun an action for false imprisonment against the Kingston bailiffs, and Winstanley was one of the arbitrators appointed by him when his case was due to come before the assizes in February.[107] Winstanley's detailed defence of Fielder was later included in the published account of the case. Among other things, Winstanley made use of a highly unusual reading of parliament's Solemn League and Covenant.[108] The covenant had been introduced in 1643 when parliament was negotiating to bring the Scots into the war, and many of the more radical supporters of parliament were uncomfortable with its religious provisions, which they feared might lead to undue clerical interference in matters of conscience. The future Leveller leader John Lilburne had, for instance, chosen to leave the army in 1645 rather than take it. The clause enjoining those who took the covenant to 'preserve and defend the King's Majesty's person and authority' was, despite the careful qualifications surrounding it, also troublesome for many. Winstanley was happy to ignore these difficulties, choosing instead to present the covenant – quite against the intentions of those who framed it – as a document designed to encourage reformation in its most far-reaching sense, and he had no difficulty in labelling those with whom he disagreed as covenant breakers. He was to do the same when he wrote to defend the Diggers' activities, arguing that the Diggers' opponents were all covenant breakers because they had been bound to assist one another in supporting the cause of religion, liberty and peace.[109] Winstanley was often willing – as in his readings of the Bible – to play freely with the meanings of constitutional documents, and in this he differed markedly from Lilburne, who was always keen to tease out the true meanings of such documents and the intentions of their authors. Winstanley may however have been acquainted with Lilburne, for the latter took over from him as counsel for John Fielder in 1650, and claimed to have been following the case from its inception.

Winstanley was joined in his defence of Fielder by a neighbour of his, Henry Bickerstaffe, who lived at Painshill on the borders of Walton and Cobham. Like Winstanley, Bickerstaffe was a former apprentice in the cloth trade, and had spent several years living in London. He moved back to the family home at Painshill before the outbreak of civil war.[110] Another local resident who came to develop close ties with Winstanley was John Coulton, a Cobham yeoman who had for many years been active in the administration of the manor and parish. His son, also named John Coulton, had served as a soldier in the Civil War and would later try to make a career as a writer of almanacs, following the example of Walton's most famous resident, the astrologer William Lilly. Coulton was, like Bickerstaffe, to join Winstanley at the start of the digging on St George's Hill, and he would become one of the most active of the Diggers, staying on until the end.[111] His friendship with Winstanley is an important reminder of the breadth of appeal of the latter's ideas. The view that the Diggers were chiefly urban radicals who descended upon an unsuspecting rural community, only to be swiftly driven away by outraged locals, has been very influential over the years, but it provides a rather misleading picture of support for the Diggers. Winstanley's acquaintances, and fellow Diggers, included settled inhabitants of his local community as well as outsiders. His core support came as much as from the rural inhabitants of his adopted parish – and no doubt reflected their concerns – as from members of London's radical religious milieu.

Winstanley's most significant encounter was, it seems, with a figure who would come to play a decisive role in the first few weeks of the digging, and who may well have helped influence the development of his ideas. This was William Everard, a voluble and unstable conjuror, former apprentice merchant taylor and soldier, who had been cashiered from the army for his alleged involvement in a plot to kill the king. He appears to have become a Baptist for a time, but like Winstanley he was soon keen to break free from the restrictions imposed by Baptist churches.[112] It is not known for certain when Winstanley first met Everard, but *Truth Lifting Up its Head* was written partly in his defence, after he had been arrested in Kingston by the town's bailiffs and been accused by local ministers of holding 'blasphemous opinions: as to deny God, and Christ, and Scriptures and prayer'.[113] Winstanley, having been in his company, had, he claimed, also been slandered by the ministers. Everard came to public attention again in March 1649, when he confronted the minister of Staines with a 'long hedginge bill' in his church, shaking the implement at him and calling on him to 'come down thou sonne of perdition come downe'.[114] It may well have been Everard who a few weeks later was responsible for thrusting a 'great burden of thorns, and bryars' into the pulpit of Walton parish church 'to stop out the Parson', and he was soon working alongside Winstanley on St George's Hill.[115] Everard's flamboyant character and his preference for confrontation over persuasion helped to ensure that in the early days of the digging he was more quickly noticed than the more self-effacing Winstanley, and many observers assumed that it was he, rather than Winstanley, who was the real leader of the Diggers.

The contacts made by Winstanley in 1648 and early 1649 were no doubt important for the evolution of his ideas, but of equal importance was the unprecedented political and economic crisis of late 1648 and early 1649. The experience of renewed fighting in the summer of 1648 had hardened attitudes in the army towards the king, who had been courted by army leaders only the previous year. The king's behaviour in encouraging royalist risings and in countenancing invasion by the Scots represented not only a betrayal of the officers' trust, but also a rejection of God's providence: in the great contest between king and parliament in the first Civil War God had, so the officers believed, granted parliament and its army a decisive victory, and the bloodshed of 1648 was therefore both unnecessary and an affront to God. Many officers and soldiers had by now come to see the king as a biblical 'Man of Blood' who must be brought to account for the blood he had needlessly caused to be shed in his kingdom. On 20 November the army presented to the House of Commons its *Remonstrance*, which called for a purge of parliament and for the trial of leading delinquents including the king. Negotiations between the king and members of parliament over the future settlement of the kingdom continued apace, and on 2 December the army occupied London. Four days later Colonel Thomas Pride and a party of soldiers prevented MPs who were suspected of supporting a treaty with the king from entering the House. The purge led swiftly to further, more radical developments. Before the end of the month an ordinance for establishing a court to try the king was read in the Commons, and was passed on 4 January. On the same day the Commons declared that 'the People are, under God, the Original of all just Power', and that 'the Commons of England, in Parliament assembled, being chosen by, and representing the People, have the Supreme Power in this Nation'.[116] On 27 January, the king was found guilty of high treason and other high crimes and was sentenced to death as 'a tyrant, traitor, murderer and public enemy to the good people of this nation'. Three days later he was executed outside the banqueting house of his palace at Whitehall. In March an act was passed to abolish the office of king, and the House of Lords was abolished because 'by too long experience' it had been found to be 'useless and dangerous to the people of England to be continued'. Two months later England was declared to be a commonwealth and free state, to be governed 'without any king or House of Lords'.[117]

Modern historians have reminded us how accidental and unplanned many of these developments were. The king's confident but naive belief in his ability to divide his enemies and rally his supporters had alienated those who had – with perhaps equal naivety – hoped that he might quietly accept the realities of his position as a defeated combatant and agree to whatever terms were imposed upon him by the civil war victors. The army leadership had been turned decisively against him and were intent on bringing him to account, but it was his refusal to plead at his trial, and his willingness to play the martyr, that ultimately determined his fate. Once the king was dead, monarchy too had to go, and so did the House of Lords. Most peers had opposed the execution of the king, and few of them had any love for the new regime, so it made no sense to keep a depleted upper house in being. The MPs who remained at Westminster after Pride's Purge, or who returned in the months following the execution of the king, held widely differing views.

Only a small number were committed republicans, and they were easily outnumbered by MPs who believed that their continued participation in government was the best guarantee against the imposition of direct military rule. England may have become a republic, but few of those who participated in the events that brought about this change would have considered themselves republicans or revolutionaries.[118]

Yet for those outside parliament, the changes that had taken place in the state seemed momentous, and for many radicals they provided hope for further, and much more extensive change. Some radical activists, most notably the Levellers, were troubled by the purge of parliament and all that followed, fearing that they had been betrayed by the army leadership and that what had taken place was little more than a military coup. The Leveller leaders were threatened with imprisonment, and Lilburne attacked the recent political changes in his aptly titled *England's New Chains Discovered*; Leveller sympathisers in the army were sowing the seeds of disaffection that would lead to the outbreak of army mutinies later in the spring. Others, however, were much more enthusiastic, and this was particularly the case with the Levellers' former allies in the separatist churches, for whom the fall of the monarchy represented their best chance of securing liberty of conscience. Religious radicals outside parliament were soon filling the press with schemes or demands for reform of the law and for the abolition of tithes – the mainstay of any national church, and a long-standing grievance for separatists – and proclaiming the end of centuries of tyranny and slavery. For many, the unprecedented fate of Charles I – which the poet George Wither saw as the moment when 'our Yoke of Norman Bondage, first was broke; And, England from her chains made free' – was an undoubted sign that the millennium was close. It was in this spirit that Winstanley produced the work that was his most remarkable to date, and the one in which he first set out his plan for occupying and digging the commons. This was his *The New Law of Righteousnes*, completed on 26 January 1649, the day before the king was sentenced and just four days before he was executed.

The New Law of Righteousnes reflected the tremendous optimism felt in radical circles and captured well the millenarian excitement of the moment. Crucially, however, it also reflected the impact of some very different developments, as a combination of grain shortages, widespread sickness and the effects of an economy still weakened by civil war threatened large numbers of people with impoverishment. The winter of 1648–9 was particularly bad, and there were reports from around the country of dearth and even famine. In London people were said to be eating dogs and cats, and many deaths were reported.[119] From Wigan came news of a 'three-corded scourge of Sword, Pestilence and Famine' afflicting those parts of Lancashire in whose 'very bowels was that great fighting, bloud-shed and breaking' of the two civil wars. Grain was short, and trade 'utterly decayed', and many families were reduced to destitution; there were 'numerous swarms of begging poore', and reports of people eating 'Carion and other unwholsome food'. Four Wigan-born Londoners, including Winstanley's kinsman James Winstanley of Gray's Inn, agreed to take responsibility for raising money in the capital for the relief of the poor of Wigan and its surrounding area.[120] Elsewhere, cattle stocks were badly affected by sickness, and James Alsop's recent suggestion that Winstanley may himself have experienced a second financial collapse towards the end of the 1640s, brought on by drought, loss of stock and high taxation, does seem very plausible.[121]

In late 1648 and 1649 numerous proposals for tackling poverty were aired, many of them the work of radicals buoyed by the prevailing spirit of change and reform; at last, it seemed, the chance had come to ensure that there should be 'no beggar in Israel'. Some urged increased charitable giving, while others sought to devise complex labour schemes which they hoped would combine effective relief of the poor with handsome financial profit for the investors and undertakers. For many, the return of commons and wastes to their proper use by the poor became a central concern. The Leveller Richard Overton had in 1647 called for enclosed or impropriated commons to be 'laid open againe to the free and common use and benefit of the poore', and this became a standard radical demand over the following four years.[122] It is likely that Winstanley was well aware that such demands were being widely made, but there was one publication in particular which must have caught his eye. This was *Light Shining in Buckinghamshire*, a work which appeared late in 1648, and which drew together deep-seated rural and provincial grievances and anti-monarchical arguments with a strikingly clear denunciation of private property. All were born equal, and none was privileged to be a lord over their own kind, but 'man following his own sensualitie' became a 'devourer of creatures, and an incloser', so that all the 'Land, Trees, Beasts, Fish, Fowle, &c' were 'inclosed into a few mercinary hands' while other people became their slaves. What was required was a return to the example of the commonwealth of ancient Israel, and to the arrangements described in the Book of Acts, where 'amongst those that received the Gospel, they were gathered into a family and had all things common; yet so, that each one was to labour and eat his own bread'.[123]

The authors of *Light Shining* apparently saw themselves as Levellers, though they seem like Winstanley to have interpreted the term Leveller in its most extreme form. The Levellers, they claimed, aimed to free all alike from slavery, and were 'most just and honest in reference to the matter of freedom: for it is the end of the redemption by Jesus, to restore all things'.[124] It was once thought that Winstanley was responsible for – or at least involved in – writing *Light Shining*, though in recent decades this suggestion has been discounted, not least on stylistic grounds. Even if he was not involved in writing it, he must have had some knowledge of the work, for it contains a number of points that find echoes in *The New Law of Righteousnes* and his later Digger tracts. *Light Shining* also suggests a familiarity on the part of the authors with Winstanley's earlier writings. It may well be the case that the authors had had some contact with Winstanley, and that the arguments advanced in their pamphlet reflected in part their understanding of his ideas as they were evolving in late 1648. References in the work to the Spirit Reason, the Golden Rule, children of light and kingly power, and the analysis of the consequences of the rise of private property and the particular way in which the Genesis story was presented in the work, strongly suggest the possibility of dialogue between the authors and Winstanley. The authors of *Light Shining* were probably also responsible for compiling *A Declaration of the Wel-Affected in the County of Buckinghamshire*, which appeared soon after digging began on St George's Hill, and which offered support to those who practised community in digging the commons. Again, this suggests contacts between them and Winstanley.[125]

In *The New Law of Righteousnes* Winstanley picked up on arguments circulating in radical circles in late 1648 and fused them with his own, very distinctive concerns, in ways that enabled him to develop a coherent programme that was quite unlike anything else seen at the time. While Winstanley may have drawn on, or at least been attentive to, the arguments of others, this work was very much his own: *The New Law of Righteousnes* was one of the most extraordinary publications to appear in England's years of revolution, and in its ambition, scope and argument it can itself be seen as truly revolutionary. Winstanley began by building on ideas that had been explored in his earlier works. He reiterated and developed the concept of the two Adams, likening the two Adams that dwelt in each individual to Esau and Jacob. The time of the first Adam was nearly done, and the law or power of righteousness – 'the one spreading power that shall remove the curse, and restore all things from the bondage every thing groans under' – was already becoming manifest. This 'rising up of Christ in sons and daughters' was 'his second comming', and, as before, Winstanley insisted that none should be excluded, for the power of righteousness would ultimately dwell in everyone, and all should learn to act righteously towards others. The work was, from its earliest pages, markedly anti-clerical and anti-formalist, and much of the argument was directed against those 'zealous Preachers and Professors in al forms' (whether of the established church or gathered congregations) whose meddling with matters of conscience interfered with true worship, and who were the greatest enemies of the ministration of the Spirit, which forsook 'all types and forms' and would 'make the greatest separation that ever was'.[126]

Not all of this was wholly original. Thomas Collier too spoke of a 'law of righteousnesse' manifesting itself in the Saints and promoting holiness and 'an external righteousnesse among men', encouraging them both to abstain from oppression, fraud and other acts of unrighteousness, and to act towards others according to the Golden Rule.[127] As before, however, fundamental differences remained, for while Collier focused his attentions on a limited body of Saints, and their relationship to the wider world, Winstanley's vision was much broader. Everyone and every thing would benefit directly from the rising power of righteousness: the spiritual light would be in every creature, and the whole creation would be purged and delivered from the curse.[128]

Additionally, Winstanley revealed psychological insights and an understanding of patterns of disadvantage and exploitation which were largely absent in the work of other radical religious writers. From the start, Winstanley honed his arguments by exploring the ways in which relations between individuals were shaped by the struggle between the two Adams, or between Jacob and Esau, within each individual. The first Adam appeared 'in every man and woman', but 'he sits down in the chair of Magistracy, in some above others'; for while 'this climbing power of self-love be in all, yet it rises not to its height in all':

> but every one that gets an authority into his hands, tyrannizes over others; as many husbands, parents, masters, magistrates, that lives after the flesh, doe carry themselves like oppressing Lords over such as are under them; not knowing that their wives, children, servants, subjects are their fellow creatures, and hath an equall priviledge to share with them in the blessing of liberty.[129]

The first Adam brought pride and envy, ignorance of the creator and 'covetousnesse after objects', as well as 'hypocrisie, subtilty, lying imagination, self-love; from whence proceeds all unrighteous outward acting'. Crucially, Winstanley now also identified it as the originator 'of particular interest, buying and selling the earth from one particular hand to another, saying, *This is mine*, upholding this particular propriety by a law of government of his own making, and thereby restraining other fellow creatures from seeking nourishment from their mother earth'. Some came to own the land while their landless neighbours were forced to work for wages. The common people 'by their labours, from the first rise of *Adam*, this particular interest upheld by the fleshes law to this day', have 'lifted up their Land-lords and others to rule in tyranny and oppression over them':

> And let all men say what they will, so long as such are Rulers as cals the Land theirs, upholding this particular propriety of *Mine and Thine*; the common-people shall never have their liberty; nor the Land ever freed from troubles, oppressions and complainings; by reason whereof the Creatour of all things is continually provoked.[130]

As with the authors of *Light Shining in Buckinghamshire*, Winstanley insisted that all were made to be lords over the creation, but not over their own kind. Everyone had been given equal freedom to till the earth and have dominion over animals, but 'this freedom is broke to pieces by the covetousnesse, and pride, and self-love, not by the law of Righteousnesse'. The earth was made 'to preserve all her children', and not to 'preserve a few covetous, proud men to live at ease, and for them to bag and barn up the treasures of the earth from others, that they might beg or starve in a fruitful land'; 'Reason requires that every man should live upon the increase of the earth comfortably.' There was, Winstanley argued, enough land in England to maintain all her inhabitants, yet 'many die for want, or live under a heavy burden of povertie all her daies'; the 'whole earth stinks, by the first *Adams* corrupt Government'. Winstanley's optimism was, however, undimmed, for the rising power of righteousness would ensure that soon 'none shall desire to have more then another, or to be Lord over other, or to lay claim to any thing as his', but 'every one shall put to their hands to till the earth, and bring up cattle, and the blessing of the earth shall be common to all; when a man hath need of any corn or cattle, take from the next store-house he meets with'.[131] Everyone would, he believed, be 'made willing to honour the King of Righteousnesse in action, being all of one heart and one mind': 'Truly we may well call this a new heaven, and a new earth, wherein dwells righteousnesse.'

There would be no need for lawyers or prisons, or for capital punishment; all outward forms of worship would cease, and the whole creation would be transformed. Even the most barren lands would be made fruitful, as the harmony between humankind and the natural world was restored, 'for the Lord wil take off the curse'.[132]

The New Law of Righteousnes was, then, an expressly millenarian work, and at its heart lay an extreme anti-formalist argument, with Winstanley looking forward confidently to the time when people, 'forsaking all forms', would come to 'worship the Father in spirit and truth; that is, to walk righteously in the Creation'. Of equal importance was Winstanley's denunciation of inequality and its causes, and his determination to see the downfall of poverty and oppression. All these arguments were intertwined, and Winstanley would have seen no logic in attempting to separate them out or to assess their relative importance. There were, he insisted, 'three doors of hope for England to escape destroying plagues': everyone should leave off running after others for knowledge and comfort and should wait instead on the Spirit Reason, they should open up their bags and barns and cease to buy and sell the land, and they should 'leave off dominion and Lordship one over another' and 'leave off imprisoning, whipping and killing; which are but the actings of the curse'. The pursuit of all 'these three particulars' was necessary for lifting the creation out of bondage; none of them was to be privileged over the others. Elsewhere in the text he explicitly linked the escape 'out of all forms and customes of the Beast, to worship the Father in spirit and truth' with the hoped for changes in social relations, for, he insisted, the former would 'more and more appear, as the earth grows up to be a common treasury'.[133]

It is as the foundation text of the digging experiment that *The New Law of Righteousnes* has become best known. Winstanley was not content just to denounce evils and express his hope that all would soon change for the better, for we also find in *The New Law of Righteousnes* the beginnings of a carefully thought-out programme for change. Like Collier, who emphasised the importance of doing as well as saying, and of action and the performance of works of 'righteous justice and equity', Winstanley insisted that 'the manifestation of a righteous heart shall be known, not by his words, but by his actions'; the time was now coming when 'men shall not talk of righteousnesse, but act righteousnesse'.[134] The course of action advocated by Winstanley came to him, so he claimed, as a vision in a trance. 'Divers matters' were revealed to him, and he heard the words '*Worke together. Eat bread together*; declare this all abroad.' This, he maintained, would 'advance the law of Righteousnesse' and help bring about the 'fall of mistical Babylon, the oppressing flesh':

> I have now obeyed the command of the Spirit that bid me declare this all abroad, I have declared it, and I wil declare it by word of mouth, I have now declared it by my pen. And when the Lord doth shew unto me the place and manner, how he wil have us that are called common people, to manure upon the common Lands, I wil then go forth and declare it in my action, to eat my bread with the sweat of my brows, without either giving or taking hire, looking upon the Land as freely mine and anothers; I have now peace in the Spirit, and I have an inward perswasion that the spirit of the poor, shal be drawn forth ere long, to act materially this Law of Righteousnesse.[135]

It is clear that Winstanley had already given a good deal of thought to how best to carry out his plan for the digging and how to overcome the many problems that he and his companions were bound to face. From the start, he made it clear that the venture would be a peaceful one, and that there would be no attempt to forcibly expropriate land. He also acknowledged that some would be reluctant to give up private property and that it might take time before they could be persuaded to accept community of goods. His response to this was thoughtful, though not wholly consistent. He accepted that property owners could, at least initially, continue to work their own lands while the poor worked together on the commons, so long as they relied only on their own labour or the labour of family and friends. On the

other hand, he refused to rule out sanctions against them. The
scriptures, as Winstanley reminded his readers, 'threaten misery
to rich men, bidding them Howl and weep', and 'surely all those
threatnings shal be materially fullfiled, for they shall be turned
out of all, and their riches given to a people that wil bring forth
better fruit, and such as they have oppressed shall inherit the
Land'. If the spirit of righteousness was bound to touch everyone
and everything, then those who chose to reject it were guilty of
forsaking Reason's law and of following their self will. Divine
judgment would not alone be sufficient. Thus anyone who tried
to continue the old ways by employing others to work the land
should lose the benefit of sonship and be forced to 'work and
eat his bread with the sweat of his own brows, not of others',
until such time as he saw the error of his ways.[136]

Laziness, refusal to work and theft would also be punished by
the loss of sonship, and those guilty of such crimes would have
land set aside to work on without assistance; any such person
would 'have a mark set upon al this time' and be a servant to
others, 'til such time as the spirit in him, make him know himself
to be equal to others in the Creation'. Everyone, he insisted, 'shal
know the Law, and every one shal obey the Law; for it shal be
writ in every ones heart; and every one that is subject to Reasons
law, shal enjoy the benefit of Sonship'. He also anticipated the
charge that community of property would lead to community of
partners, and made it clear that 'immoderate lust after strange
flesh' was associated with the rule of the first rather than the
second Adam; the reign of the second would be marked instead
by chastity. Winstanley did not dwell at any great length on the
problems likely to confront attempts to establish community,
but the very mention of them shows that he was aware that the
chosen path would be a difficult one. His essentially optimistic
message, and belief that the whole creation would be swept
up by the rising power of Christ, was clearly tempered by the
realisation that the Beast would not be vanquished quickly or
easily; and for all Winstanley's refusal to countenance violence,
he does appear to have realised that the Digger experiment could
never succeed as a wholly voluntaristic enterprise.[137]

It is in relation to the role of the common people that Winstanley provided some of his most powerful insights. The poor should not just be seen as an object of pity, for the part they played in upholding the curse had also to be addressed. Private property, and the poverty, inequality and exploitation attendant upon it, was, like the corruption of religion, kept in being not only by the rich but also by those who worked for them. Winstanley's vision enjoined him to declare that 'Whosoever it is that labours in the earth, for any person or persons, that lifts up themselves as Lords & Rulers over others, and that doth not look upon themselves equal to others in the Creation, The hand of the Lord shall be upon that labourer.' The poor should not only therefore be encouraged to throw in their lot with the new society, but they must be made to face up to their complicity in maintaining the existing social arrangements: they should, in particular, acknowledge that 'this miserie the poor people have brought upon themselves, by lifting up particular interest, by their labours'. Winstanley's declaration to the poor was direct and uncompromising:

> Therefore you dust of the earth, that are trod under foot, you poor people, that makes both schollars and rich men, your opressours by your labours. Take notice of your priviledge, the Law of Righteousnesse is now declared.
>
> If you labour the earth, and work for others that lives at ease, and follows the waies of the flesh by your labours, eating the bread which you get by the sweat of your brows, not their own: Know this, that the hand of the Lord shal break out upon every such hireling labourer, and you shal perish with the covetous rich men, that have held, and yet doth hold the Creation under the bondage of the curse.[138]

Winstanley acknowledged that working the wastes in common, while leaving private estates untouched, could bring only partial change. The mass withdrawal of labour was therefore always also part of his plan. A wage strike would bring large numbers of poor people on to the commons to practise community, and would at the same time effectively deprive the rich of any land they could not farm by themselves. The rich would thus be reduced to the status of peasant proprietors or family producers, and this would in turn provide them with greater incentives for abandoning their holdings and joining with 'this common interest of earthly community'.[139] It was a bold plan and, as Winstanley appreciated, one that had never before been tried. It remained to be seen how quickly the English could be persuaded to abandon private property and embrace community.

3
Winstanley the Digger

Not a full yeere since, being quiet at my work, my heart was filled with sweet thoughts, and many things were revealed to me which I never read in books, nor heard from the mouth of any flesh, and when I began to speak of them, some people could not bear my words, and amongst those revelations this was one, *That the earth shall be made a common Treasury of livelihood to whole mankind, without respect of persons*; and I had a voice within me bad me declare it all abroad, which I did obey, for I declared it by word of mouth wheresoever I came, then I was made to write a little book called, *the new Law of righteousnesse*, and therein I declared it; yet my mind was not at rest, because nothing was acted, and thoughts run in me, that <u>words and writings</u> were all nothing, and must die, for <u>action is the life of all, and if thou dost</u> <u>not act, thou dost nothing.</u> Within a little time I was made obedient to the word in that particular likewise; for I tooke my spade and went and broke the ground upon *George-hill* in Surrey, thereby declaring freedome to the Creation, and that the earth must be set free from intanglements of Lords and Landlords, and that it shall become a common Treasury to all, as it was first made and given to the sonnes of men.[1]

With these words, written in the last week of August 1649, Winstanley described the beginnings of the Digger venture. Work began on Sunday 1 April, when a small group of women and men started digging and sowing vegetables on the wastes of St George's Hill in the parish of Walton on Thames.[2] For the next twelve months Winstanley's energies would be devoted to establishing Digger communities, advancing and defending the Digger cause in print and attempting to stave off the destruction of the chief Digger settlements in Walton and Cobham. Before the occupation of the commons began Winstanley was a settled householder and farmer in Cobham, who would have been known and respected locally as the son-in-law of the

prominent surgeon William King, and who was one of the few
Cobham inhabitants to be described by their neighbours as a
gentleman.[3] Now all this was cast aside as he set out to lead
a movement of the poor which would, he believed, transform
society, advance reformation and change human behaviour in
wholly unprecedented ways. What he and his companions had
begun on St George's Hill (or as they chose to call it, George
Hill) would, he hoped, shortly spread to the rest of England and
then throughout the world.

The Diggers announced their intentions in a manifesto entitled
The True Levellers Standard Advanced, which drew directly
on the arguments advanced by Winstanley in *The New Law of
Righteousnes*. In the beginning of time the great creator Reason
had made the earth to be a common treasury; man had been
given dominion over the birds, beasts and fishes, but 'not one
word was spoken in the beginning, that one branch of mankind
should rule over another'. As 'human fleshe (that King of Beasts)'
fell to delighting in the objects of the creation, selfish imagination
took possession of the five senses and, along with covetousness,
'did set up one man to teach and rule over another': 'and thereby
the Spirit was killed, and man was brought into bondage, and
became a greater slave to such of his owne kind, then the Beasts of
the field were to him'. The earth was then hedged into inclosures
by teachers and rulers, 'and the others were made servants and
slaves'; and what had first been made as a 'common Store-house
for all' was now 'bought and sold, and kept in the hands of a
few'. The great Creator was thus 'mightily dishonoured, as if
he were a respecter of persons, delighting in the comfortable
livelihood of some, and rejoicing in the miserable poverty and
straights of others. From the beginning it was not so.'[4]

Covetousness had led people to accept outward teachers and
rulers and to neglect the Law of Righteousness in their hearts,
'which is the pure light of Reason'. But the great Creator or Spirit
Reason would only be rejected and trodden under foot for a
limited time, and so the earth was bound to become a common
treasury again, 'for all the Prophecies of Scriptures and Reason
are Circled here in this Community, and mankind must have the
Law of Righteousnesse once more writ in his heart, and all must

be made of one heart, and one mind'. Esau, the man of flesh or powers of the earth, who had made a servant of Jacob, the younger brother or spirit of meekness, now faced his downfall.[5]

As in *The New Law of Righteousnes*, Winstanley made clear his disavowal of violence. He and his companions would, by labouring the earth and eating together, and refusing to give or take hire, endeavour 'by the power of Reason, the Law of righteousnesse in us', to 'lift up the Creation from the bondage of Civill Propriety, which it groans under'. By digging on St George's Hill and the neighbouring waste grounds, they would, he claimed,

lay the Foundation of making the Earth a common Treasury for all, both Rich and Poor, That every one that is born in the Land, may be fed by the Earth his Mother that brought him forth, according to the Reason that rules in the Creation. Not inclosing any part into any particular hand, but all as one man, working together, and feeding together as Sons of one Father, members of one Family; not one Lording over another, but all looking upon each other, as equalls in the Creation.[6]

In doing this they would glorify the maker, who loved his whole creation and did not make the earth for only a few to enjoy. Private property was the curse, obtained by oppression, murder or theft, and those who assumed that the land belonged rightly to lords and landlords 'consent still to hold the Creation down under that bondage it groans under'. Landlords were deceivers, who had persuaded the poor to lift them up through wage labour or the payment of rent, or who 'out-reached the plain-hearted in buying and selling'; they monopolised offices and places of trust, and enslaved the poor through oppressive laws of their own making. Private property brought wars and division, which would cease once people were 'united by common community of livelihood into Onenesse'. The command to work together and eat together had been declared in writing, and now Winstanley and his companions were declaring it in action, by digging and sowing the commons and refusing to work for hire. They had, he claimed, 'been made to sit down and count what it may cost us in undertaking such a work, and we know the full sum', but they had no fears of prison or death: they were resolved to continue,

> For by this work we are assured, and Reason makes it appear to others, that bondage shall be removed, tears wiped away, and all poor people by their righteous labours shall be relieved, and freed from Poverty and Straits; For in this work of Restoration, there will be no beggar in Israel.[7]

In *The True Levellers Standard*, as in *The New Law of Righteousnes* before it, Winstanley's denunciation of teachers and professors comes through as strongly as his denunciation of landowners, and as before it would be unhelpful to try to disentangle his anti-formalist arguments from his advocacy of communist social transformation. With the rise of universal liberty and the restoration of all things, the earth would be as free from forms and customs as it would be from private property; the need to reject the teachings of others, and all attempts to impose worthless forms, remained as pressing, and as necessary to the work of restoration, as the need to throw off the power of landlords. The corruption of religion went back to the rise of the first Adam, and so religion had to be restored to its perfect, prelapsarian state. The 'teaching and ruling power' had been an oppressor even in the time of Moses, and Moses's law was 'a Language lapped up in Types, Sacrifices, Forms, and Customs, which was a weak time'; there could not, for Winstanley, be any sense in emulating the ancient commonwealth of Israel or seeking to impose Mosaic law, in the way that many religious radicals were beginning to advocate.[8]

The True Levellers Standard was framed as a declaration 'to the Powers of England, and to all the powers of the world', and so its focus differed in significant ways from that of *The New Law of Righteousnes*. Throughout the work there can be found criticism of parliament and the army that echoes – and in places matches in intensity – the criticism directed at the new commonwealth regime by the Levellers. The common people had been 'filled with good words from Pulpits and Councell Tables, but no good deeds': 'while they wait for liberty, behold greater bondage comes insteed of it'. The powers of England

had 'promised to make this People a Free People, yet thou hast
so handled the matter, through thy self-seeking humour, That
thou hast wrapped us up more in bondage, and oppression lies
heavier upon us'. Covenants and oaths had been taken, but
people were imprisoned for pursuing the covenant; ordinances
had been made to cast down oppressing laws, but 'Self-will and
Prerogative power, is the great standing Law'; and promises and
protestations that had been made to make the land a free nation
had as yet no discernable effect.[9]

Two important new lines of argument were introduced, which
we find repeated in many of the publications issued by the Diggers
over the coming year. First, we see Winstanley making use of
Norman Yoke theories – that body of radical, and popular, ideas
in which current social and political inequalities were explained
by reference to the destruction of native liberties at the time of
the Norman Conquest.[10] The Norman Conquest was 'the last
inslaving Conquest which the enemy got over Israel', and all the
kings, lords, office holders and freeholders who followed were
but the successors of the Conqueror, his officers and common
soldiers. Now, as the enslaved English began to seek their liberty,
attempts were being made to impose the Norman power ever
more forcibly over them: despite all promises to make the English
a free people, the 'powers of England' still 'lift up that Norman
yoke, and slavish tyranny, and holds the people as much in
bondage, as the Bastard Conqueror himselfe, and his Councell of
War'.[11] In incorporating Norman Yoke theories into his writings,
Winstanley was again paying heed to Leveller arguments and
those of other radical critics of the new regime.[12] The authors of
Light Shining in Buckinghamshire, who had produced a second
instalment of their work in March 1649, also made much of
the continuance of the Norman Yoke and complained of the
'Arbitrary Powers erected anew'; they emphasised the pressing
need to strip away the remnants of Norman power, and called
on common soldiers to take responsibility for this if parliament
and the army officers failed to act.[13]

Related to this line of argument was Winstanley's new focus on
contract and on the obligations owed by those in power to those
below the ranks of the gentry. Promises had been made to the

common people in exchange for their assistance against the king in the Civil War: the people had bought their freedom with their 'Money, in Taxes, Free-Quarter and Blood-shed', and parliament and army were bound by their 'Covenants and Promises' to fulfil their side of the bargain. The people, Winstanley declared, had not 'laid out their moneyes, and shed their blood, that their Landlords, the *Norman* power, should still have its liberty and freedome to rule in Tyranny in his Lords, Landlords, Judges, Justices, Bayliffs, and State-Servants', but that 'the oppressed might be set free, prison-doors opened, and the poor peoples hearts comforted by an universall consent of making the earth a Common Treasury'.[14] Significantly, these arguments showed clear echoes of traditional languages of social protest and discontent, languages that would have been familiar to the rural poor whose support Winstanley most hoped to attract.[15] Like the arguments drawing on popular notions of morality and bodily necessity, which would become of increasing importance to Winstanley in his later Digger writings, they suggest a subtle shift in emphasis in favour of prioritising the social case for the occupation of the commons. This too reflected frequently voiced radical concerns and argument in the months following the execution of the king. *More Light Shining in Buckingham-shire* had also targeted those 'Tyrants, called lords of manors', and the manorial courts, fines and heriots through which they continued to oppress the bulk of the rural population; the poor who had fought in the wars had, they argued, 'come home again, as very slaves as at the first'.[16] Later in the year, the authors of a Hertfordshire *Declaration or Representation* complained of the 'small requital' that the people had obtained for their services and expense in support of parliament. Most of the people had supported parliament in the wars, while most of their oppressors, the 'great men of the Nation', had supported the king. The latter continued to enjoy their privileges, and to keep the former in slavery by means of 'base tenures, fines, heriots, fealty, homage &c and by tithes, and the Lawes in the Norman Tongue'.[17] All these authors agreed that although the king had gone, kingly power remained, particularly in rural areas. The concept of kingly power was one that Winstanley would make very much his own in the coming months.

Although the influence on Winstanley of Leveller and Leveller-related pamphlets is clear, it is possible that his increasing focus on rural grievances also reflected the views of others who joined him on St George's Hill, and who were keen to see their concerns articulated in the first Digger manifesto. If this was the case, then it demonstrates that from the start the experiment had a quite practical, as well as symbolic, purpose, and that early support for the venture was by no means restricted to the narrow base of religious radicalism. For some the religious message may have been most important, but for others it seems likely that the case for digging was as much about questions of subsistence, the social costs of war and dearth, and the inequalities that survived in post-civil-war England. Patterns of support for Winstanley's experiment would appear to bear this out.

The title page of *The True Levellers Standard Advanced* listed the names of 15 of those, including Winstanley, who were 'beginning to plant and manure the waste land upon George Hill'. Although women were involved in the digging from the start, only the names of men were noted on the title page, and the practice of excluding women's names would be continued in later Digger publications. Many of the names in *The True Levellers Standard* were, like the names appended to later Digger pamphlets and manifestos, local ones. Although there are many problems involved in trying to identify individual Diggers – most of whom had common names – recent research suggests that around a third of Winstanley's companions were from the locality, and that the largest number of these came from the parish of Cobham. Local support was not only evident in the early stages of the experiment. New recruits from in and around Cobham continued to join the Diggers throughout the year spent working the commons, and it seems that the majority of the most active and committed Diggers were local inhabitants.[18] Winstanley was clearly as adept at appealing to rural inhabitants – both middling sorts and poor – as he was to the kind of religious radicals from London and elsewhere who might seem the most likely participants in this experiment in radical activism.[19]

The earliest reports of the Diggers' activities on St George's Hill suggested that they had started their work on 'that side [of] the Hill next to Campe Close'.[20] The name 'Camp Close' was sometimes said to refer to the iron age encampment overlooking the steep southern slopes of the hill, but it seems to have been used most often to describe the flat of the common between the encampment and the boundary of the royal park at Oatlands.[21] The land around was notoriously barren, as Winstanley was quick to acknowledge. If the heaths of St George's Hill, which in 1650 were dismissed by parliament's surveyors as 'extreame barren being nothing but a bare heath & sandy ground', could be made fruitful, it would be proof of the divine blessing the Diggers hoped for. But millenarian optimism was not alone sufficient to bring success to their venture. It seems clear that the Diggers – true to the local origins of so many of them – were well aware of the techniques needed to grow crops on such unpromising soils. They followed profitable and well-established local practice by engaging in spade husbandry, planting root crops and denshiring the heath.[22] Henry Sanders, the local official who first reported on the Diggers' activities, described how they began by digging and sowing the ground with parsnips, carrots and beans on the first Sunday of their work, while on the Monday they fired around ten acres of heathland and continued all day at digging. They had, he claimed, also intended to put two or three ploughs to work, but were unable to do so until they acquired seed corn at Kingston on the following Saturday.[23]

Winstanley and his companions had expected opposition, but they may not have anticipated quite how violent the response to their activities would be. St George's Hill was part of the extensive, unstinted commons of the manor of Walton, and Walton inhabitants who made use of the hill to graze their sheep and cattle were clearly alarmed by the sudden arrival of the Diggers. Sanders's report pointedly made mention of the fact that the first Diggers were 'all living att Cobham', and the immediate response of Walton's inhabitants and manorial tenants was to treat this incursion from a neighbouring parish in the traditional way, by resorting to concerted communal action. The Diggers' aims were no doubt also misunderstood – Sanders was probably repeating local rumour when he misleadingly stated that the Diggers intended to force the neighbouring people to come to the hill and work, and that they were threatening to cut the legs off any cattle that came too close to the new plantation. His suggestion that 'they give out, they will bee four or five thousand within 10 dayes' may well however have been an accurate reflection of the optimism felt by the Diggers when they embarked on their project.[24]

Evidence of the nature and extent of opposition can be pieced together from a variety of sources, including Winstanley's own writings, newsbook reports and legal documents. The first clash, according to Winstanley, who drew up a list of the Diggers' 'remarkable sufferings' in anticipation of later Quaker sufferings accounts, came when 'divers of the diggers' were carried to Walton's parish church, where they were struck 'by the bitter professors and rude multitude'; eventually they were freed by a Justice of the Peace. On the second occasion, a crowd of 'above a hundred rude people' took away their spades and carried the Diggers firstly to prison at Walton and then to a JP at Kingston, 'who presently dismissed them'. This crowd was, significantly, said to have been led by John Taylor, a Walton inhabitant and sheep farmer who lived near St George's Hill, and who must have felt particularly threatened by the Digger occupation of the commons on which his livelihood depended. A newly built Digger house on the hill was then pulled down by 'the dragonly enemy', and the Diggers' spades and hoes broken into pieces.[25]

The report written by Henry Sanders was intended for the Council of State, and was read there on 16 April. The Council, mindful of Sanders's warning that 'itt is feared they have some designe in hand', wrote immediately to Lord Fairfax, the commander of the army, and to Surrey's Justices of the Peace, urging that action be taken against the Diggers. As the council informed Fairfax:

Although the pretence of their being there by them avowed may seeme very ridiculous, yet that conflux of people may be a beginning whence

things of a greater & more dangerous consequence may grow to the
disturbance of the Peace & quiet of the Comonwealth.

They recommended that the lord general send 'some force of
Horse' to Cobham to disperse the Diggers and prevent them from
returning to the hill, so that 'a malignant & disaffected party may
not under Colour of such ridiculous people have an opportunity
to rendezvous themselves in order to a greater mischiefe'.[26]

Fairfax responded by ordering two troops of horse to
investigate. One of them was the lord general's own troop,
commanded by Captain John Gladman. Gladman, a Baptist,
was quick to play down the significance of what he found. On
approaching St George's Hill he had sent four troopers ahead
to 'bring certaine intelligence to me'. On the way there the
soldiers encountered Winstanley and Everard, who agreed to
travel to London to explain their actions to Fairfax. Having
questioned his soldiers, and spoken to his fellow officers at
Kingston, Gladman decided that there was no need for him to
march any further that day. There had, he concluded, been no
more than 'twentie of them together since they first undertooke
the businesse'; Everard was 'no other than a madd man', and
Fairfax would be 'glad to bee rid of them againe'. The business,
he concluded, 'is not worth the writing nor yet taking nottis
of: I wonder the Council of State should be so abused with
informations'.[27] His visit to St George's Hill the following day
appeared to confirm his first impressions. He found only four
men digging: 'they have digged in all about an Acre of Land,
but it is trampled down by the Country people, who would not
suffer them to dig one day more'.[28]

The digging experiment might well have ended there, brought
swiftly to a halt by local opposition and the actions of the army.
But Captain Gladman had been instructed to bring Winstanley
and Everard before the lord general, and this provided the Diggers
with a glorious opportunity to publicise their activities. On 20
April they appeared before Fairfax and other senior officers at
Whitehall and – again in anticipation of later Quaker practice –
they refused to remove their hats before a fellow creature. Everard
made a lengthy speech, justifying and explaining the Diggers'

THE
Declaration and Standard

Of the *Levellers* of *England* ;
Delivered in a Speech to his Excellency the Lord Gen. *Fairfax,*
on *Friday* last at White-Hall, by Mr. *Everard,* a late Member of the
Army, and his Prophesie in reference thereunto ; shewing what will
befall the Nobility and Gentry of this Nation, by their submitting to
community ; With their invitation and promise unto the people, and
their proceedings in *Windsor* Park, *Oatlands* Park, and severall other
places ; also, the Examination and confession of the said Mr. *Everard*
before his Excellency, the manner of his deportment with his Hat on,
and his severall speeches and expressions, when he was commanded
to put it off. Together with a List of the severall Regiments of Horse
and Foot that have cast Lots to go for *Ireland.*

Imprinted at *London,* for *G. Laurenson, Aprill* 2 3. 1649.

Winstanley and Everard meet Lord General Fairfax at Whitehall, 20 April 1649. From *The Declaration and Standard of the Levellers of England* (1649).

activities, and this was transcribed and rushed into print as *The Declaration and Standard of the Levellers of England.*[29] Soon almost every available journalist had descended on Cobham, and weekly newsbooks were full of stories about 'the new fangled people that begin to dig on St George's Hill', who had returned

to the hill at the first opportunity. The reports varied greatly in
terms of accuracy and seriousness. *The Moderate*, a newsbook
sympathetic to the Levellers, provided without any hostile
comment a lengthy extract from Everard's speech before Fairfax,
while *The Kingdomes Faithfull and Impartiall Scout* reported
on a bad-tempered exchange between an unnamed Digger and
a 'modest Gentleman', which ended with the gentleman boxing
the Digger's ears and the latter threatening to sow the ground
with hempseed.[30] The clandestine royalist newsbook *The Man
in the Moon* spoke with wild inaccuracy about 'Everards digging
upon Kingstone Common', *Mercurius Pragmaticus* laughed at
the Diggers' intention 'to have converted Oatlands Park into a
Wildernesse, and preach Liberty to the oppressed Deer', and
Perfect Occurences described their plans (never mentioned by
Winstanley) to dig on Newmarket, Hounslow and Hampstead
heaths.[31] Very soon several newsbooks were reporting that the
'new plantation' on St George's Hill was 'quite re-leveled, and
their new Creation utterly destroyed, and by the Country people
thereabouts, they are driven away', and press interest in the
Diggers quickly evaporated.[32]

The brief flurry of press interest may well have been troubling
to Winstanley. Not only did many newsbooks disparage the
Diggers' aims (they were described as 'a distracted, crack brained
people', 'wanting reason and parts', and 'a pure contradiction
of themselves'), but two additional problems emerged.[33] The
first was to do with William Everard. Almost every newsbook
writer assumed that he was the leader of the digging, and
he seems to have done his best to confirm this by seizing the
limelight in the meeting with Fairfax. Winstanley's name was
rarely mentioned, and when it was it was usually as Everard's
companion or associate. 'Prophet Everet' was treated derisively
by many newsbook writers, and was portrayed as someone
'rewarded with the gift of Lunacy, instead of Revelation'; his
grandstanding risked reducing Winstanley's serious vision to
a matter of ridicule.[34] We cannot be sure what happened next
– whether Everard quickly lost interest in the digging venture
or whether Winstanley re-asserted his authority in a decisive
fashion – but very soon Everard had left George Hill. By the

time signatures were added to a second Digger pamphlet issued at the end of May, his name was absent, and he seems never to have returned to the digging.

In August Everard turned up at Bradfield in Berkshire, where the rector John Pordage had gathered about him a peaceful community influenced by the ideas of Jacob Boehme.[35] Pordage recalled waking in his bedchamber in the middle of the night to be confronted by 'a spirit in the shape of Everard, with his wearing apparel, Band, Cuffs, Hat, &c', who 'after the sudden drawing of the Bed-Curtains, seemed to walk once thorow the Chamber very easily, and so disappeared'. This was but one of three 'dreadful Apparitions' to appear that night, being quickly followed by spirits 'in the form of a Gyant' and 'in the shape of a great Dragon' with 'great teeth, and open jaws, whence he oft ejected fire against me'.[36] The next time Everard was at Bradfield Pordage fell into a trance and was seen running out of the church 'bellowing like a Bull'. Clearly Everard was adept at making an impression wherever he went. In September 1650 he was spotted in London 'in frantick posture', and the last we hear of 'Ranting Everard' was in 1651 as a prisoner in London's Bridewell, where orders were given for his transfer to Bethlem hospital as a result of his 'distracted' and 'outragious' behaviour.[37]

The second problem was one that Winstanley had possibly not anticipated. This was connected with the title of the Digger manifesto, *The True Levellers Standard Advanced*, which reached booksellers' shelves in late April.[38] The work's title has sometimes puzzled scholars, since elsewhere in his writings Winstanley never used the term 'True Levellers' to describe the Diggers. Some have wondered whether the title was chosen by the publisher rather the author, possibly as a means of boosting sales. All the evidence, however, suggests that the text supplied to the printer, including the title page, was in Winstanley's own hand. The meaning of his title may, however, have been misunderstood. Elsewhere in his Digger writings Winstanley came to refer to Christ as 'the true and faithfull Leveller', 'the head Leveller' or even as 'the greatest, first, and truest Leveller that ever was spoke of in the world'; he also referred to the 'true Levelling which Christ would work at his more glorious appearance'.[39] It

is quite possible that in choosing a title Winstanley was wanting
to announce the raising or advancing of the standard of Christ,
the 'True Leveller', rather than declaring that he and his fellow
Diggers were 'True Levellers'. The fact that the title bore no
apostrophe, as was common in seventeenth-century practice,
meant that alternative meanings were always possible.

The journalists who descended on St George's Hill towards the
end of April had no doubts about what Winstanley had meant.
Winstanley and his companions were immediately labelled 'the
true Levellers, as they call themselves under their standard', and
the name has stuck.[40] Generations of historians have debated
the significance of the name – were the Diggers, for instance,
seeking to place themselves on or to the left of the Levellers,
and did the choice of name imply criticism of the mainstream
Leveller movement? In some modern editions of Winstanley's
writings the missing apostrophe has been silently reinstated and
the title of the Digger manifesto has become an unambiguous
The True Levellers' Standard Advanced.[41] But for the Diggers to
choose to call themselves true Levellers, or to claim to be even
more true to the principles of Levellerism than were the Leveller
leaders, would have been unhelpful in April 1649. Four leading
Levellers – John Lilburne, William Walwyn, Richard Overton
and Thomas Prince – had been arrested and brought before the
Council of State only days before the Diggers began work on St
George's Hill, and plans were in place to proceed against them as
traitors. It was on this occasion that Lilburne famously put his
ear to the door and claimed to hear Oliver Cromwell ('I am sure
of it', he later wrote) 'thumping his fists upon the Councel Table'
and exclaiming, "I tell you Sir, you have no other way to deale
with these men but to break them in pieces"'.[42] Army discontent
was growing, and was closely connected with the Leveller
campaign. Soldiers in Colonel Whalley's regiment, which was
quartered in London, mutinied on 24 April, and on the 26th,
less than a week after Everard and Winstanley had been brought
before Fairfax at Whitehall, six soldiers from the regiment were
condemned to death. One of them, Robert Lockyer, a known
Leveller sympathiser, was executed on 27 April after Fairfax
had refused pleas for clemency. Thousands attended his funeral,

many wearing ribbons in the sea-green colours associated with the Levellers. Within a short time mutinies had spread to Salisbury, Sussex and Oxfordshire, and at Banbury soldiers were uniting behind demands for the implementation of the Leveller *Agreement of the People*. Loyal units of the army marched from London under Fairfax and Cromwell and overwhelmed around 900 mutineers at Burford in Oxfordshire, where three soldiers were executed. William Thompson, one of the most committed of the 'physical force' Levellers, remained at large for a time with two troops of horse, but on 17 May he was killed in a skirmish in woods near Wellingborough.[43] Reports also reached London that one of the leaders of the mutineers in Oxfordshire was none other than William Everard, though this was apparently a case of mistaken identity.[44] The Diggers, faced with violent local opposition to their venture on St George's Hill, were keen to gain the army's protection and would not have wanted to provoke Fairfax into acting against them. Winstanley sought to emphasise the Diggers' peaceable aims and he went out of his way to praise Fairfax for his moderation. It seems unlikely that he would have chosen to launch the Digger experiment by proclaiming it as the work of Levellers of any kind.

The confusion over the Diggers' name had consequences for both Diggers and Levellers. On the one hand it could seem to confirm the Council of State's fears that 'the Malignant & disaffected party' might turn the digging on St George's Hill into a 'dangerous insurrection'.[45] It also gave government supporters the opportunity to falsely link the Levellers to support for community of property. The author of *The Discoverer*, ignoring all Leveller protestations in favour of protecting private property, drew solemnly on Winstanley's writings to demonstrate to his readers that the Levellers were communists, atheists and anti-scripturalists who also asserted that 'Reason is God, and out of this Reason came the whole Creation'.[46] Similarly the newsbook *Perfect Occurrences*, reporting on Cromwell's account of the 'seasonable and happy reducing of the Levellers', alleged that among the Levellers' designs had been a plan 'to have proportioned all mens Estates by way of Community'.[47] Such wilful misinterpretation helped neither group, and Winstanley would not have been happy to see the Levellers, for whom he clearly had a good deal of sympathy, embarrassed in this way. The Levellers responded to the libels by denying, quite reasonably, any connection with Winstanley's programme. Walwyn's son-in-law Humphrey Brooke pointed out that some of the most damning citations in *The Discoverer* were from 'a Book none of us own, called, *The New Law of Righteousness*', written by a 'certain man to whom we have no Relation'; for good measure Brooke also suggested that the accusation of denial of a deity was probably as false in Winstanley's case as it was in theirs.[48] In June John Lilburne concluded his *Legal Fundamental Liberties* with an attack on *The Discoverer* for attempting to father 'upon me, &c. all the erronious tenents of the poor Diggers at George Hill', as set down in their *True Levellers Standard* and *New Law of Righteousnes*.[49]

We should not make too much of these disavowals. The Levellers' views on private property were never wholly consistent: Lilburne was probably the most outspoken in his opposition to the 'conceit of levelling of propriety and Magistracie', Overton acknowledged the advantages of opening up impropriated common land and turning it over to the poor (a move that would have infringed the property rights of landowners), while Walwyn never convincingly repudiated the accusation that he had – in theory at least – some sympathy for the idea of community of property. Their agreed position, which may have been the result of compromise within the movement, seems to have been that community of property was in itself neither a good nor a bad thing; the primitive Christians were believed to have practised it, so it could obviously not be condemned out of hand. Community was, however, something that could only ever be introduced on the basis of 'universal assent'; and unless such assent was first given no person or government had any right to attempt to introduce it. It seems very unlikely that they thought that it ever would, or should be introduced, and they made clear that they had no intention of advocating its implementation.[50] The Levellers defended property rights against those who threatened them, and they did so principally in terms of what Brian Manning has defined as the defence of small property against big property.[51] The name that the Levellers went under was not one they had chosen for themselves, and they had constantly to try to refute the charge that they intended social levelling.[52] The frequent reference to private property in their writings may have been as much a reflection of their defensiveness in the face of the unfair criticism their name attracted as it was a positive statement of principle.[53] When they distanced themselves from the Diggers, it was quite specifically in relation to the untruths contained in *The Discoverer*, and it need not be seen as an outright condemnation of Digger aims. All that the Levellers were doing was to deny that the Diggers' aims were theirs, and to point out that it was misleading for their opponents to suggest that they were.

In the 1940s and 1950s, when Soviet interpretations of the English Revolution were at their most influential, the Levellers fell out of favour among some sections of the left, and a sharp distinction was sometimes drawn between the Levellers' supposedly 'petty-bourgeois' ideology and Winstanley's more thorough-going 'anticipation of historical materialism and scientific communism'. The Levellers were seen to be constrained by the shifting and unstable position of the class they represented, and it was assumed that they were doomed to failure.[54] Much was made of their failure to unite with the Diggers against their common enemies, and when they disavowed Digger aims they were accused of 'savagely attacking' the Diggers.[55] Although such views have not wholly disappeared, historians of the left are today much more likely to portray the Levellers as genuine revolutionaries, and few would now condemn them for not being Diggers or 'True Levellers'.[56] The two groups were simply different, as Winstanley would have appreciated, and as soon as he got the chance he took steps to ensure that there would no longer be any confusion over names. When a new edition of the first Digger manifesto appeared, the title *True Levellers Standard* was quietly dropped, and was replaced with the safer title *A Declaration to the Powers of England*.[57] In referring to his companions on George Hill, Winstanley reverted to using another name that newsbook writers had first applied to them –

that of 'Digger'. The term 'true Leveller' would henceforth only be used in reference to Christ.[58]

The Levellers and Diggers from then on formed two recognisably distinct groups, and it was probably coincidental that both these names had been applied some years earlier to enclosure rioters in the Midland Rising of 1607.[59] But the two groups were in many respects complimentary, and it is no accident that some of the earliest documented support for the Digger venture came from Buckinghamshire, from self-proclaimed Levellers linked to the *Light Shining* pamphlets. At a meeting of 'Middle Sort of men' in Aylesbury in May, several resolutions were adopted, including ones supporting the poor in digging the commons and joining 'in community in Gods way, as those [in] *Acts* 2'. These Buckinghamshire 'Wel-affected' also agreed to support the poor in felling woods growing on the commons.[60] The latter resolution reflected the practical side of the Digger venture which was becoming increasingly evident in the weeks and months following the initial occupation of St George's Hill.

In the Diggers' second manifesto, which was issued in May and signed by 45 Diggers or Digger sympathisers, Winstanley spelt out plans to cut and sell wood on the commons in order to raise funds for purchasing food, corn, agricultural implements and other necessary materials. He continued to denounce the iniquities of the current social and economic system: buying and selling was, for instance, 'the great cheat, that robs and steals the Earth one from another', making 'some Lords, others Beggers, some Rulers, others to be ruled', and making 'great Murderers and Theeves to be imprisoners, and hangers of little ones, or of sincere-hearted men'.[61] But less was now being said about the imminent transformation of the whole of society, and Winstanley's attention was turning more to the need to ensure the success of the St George's Hill colony and any that might follow.[62] In Digger pamphlets issued in the spring and early summer, much greater emphasis was placed on arguments deriving from necessity, as Winstanley sought to demonstrate the utility of allowing the poor to work together to feed themselves in a time of scarcity. He played down the threat posed by digging to other landholders, and quietly dropped from his writings his earlier, provocative demands for the mass withdrawal of wage labour. The Diggers would peacefully occupy the commons, providing sustenance for themselves and their families, while the gentry enjoyed their own lands, so that elder and younger brother might 'live free and quiet one by, and with another, not burthening one another in this land of our Nativity'.[63]

The shift in tactics had some measure of success, since Winstanley appears at least to have persuaded Fairfax of the sincerity and peaceful intentions of the Diggers. In one of the more curious episodes of the digging, the lord general made a detour to visit St George's Hill on his return to London after the defeat of the Levellers at Burford. He spoke at length to Winstanley, who was one of about twelve Diggers present, and he inspected the Diggers' plantation. Winstanley was later able to praise Fairfax for his 'mildnesse and moderation', and he seemed confident that the lord general would deal with any of his soldiers who took it upon themselves to threaten the Diggers.[64] Despite this, the violence continued, as Walton's parishioners and manorial tenants made further concerted attempts to recover their commons from Winstanley and his companions. In late May, the Diggers' attempts to fetch wood from Stoke common met with violent resistance from locals, and a cart was destroyed and a horse cut on its back with a bill.[65] Only a few days after Fairfax's visit, two Diggers – a man and a boy – were attacked by soldiers who were quartered near the hill. In Winstanley's words, the soldiers,

before any word of provocation was spoken to them, fell upon these two, beating the boy, and took away his coat off his back, and some linnen and victualls that they had, beating and wounding the man very dangerously, and fired our house.

It was, Winstanley insisted, 'a strange and Heathenish practise' that 'the soulderie should meddle with naked men, peaceable men, Countrymen, that meddled not with the souldiers businesse, nor offered any wrong to them in word or deed'.[66] On 11 June the Diggers were victims of a customary form of popular protest, in what Winstanley described as the 'bloudie and unchristian acting of William Starr and John Taylor of Walton, with divers men in womens apparel'. Taylor had been a leader of the crowd actions against the Diggers in April, and Starr was another local farmer with interests in the commons around St George's Hill.[67] As four of the Diggers were preparing ground for the winter season, they were said by Winstanley to have been approached by the two freeholders on horseback, with the 'men in womens apparell' following behind. Each of them carried 'a staffe or club',

> and as soon as they came to the diggers, would not speak like men, but like bruit beasts that have no understanding, they fell furiously upon them, beating and striking those foure naked men, beating them to the ground, breaking their heads, and sore bruising their bodies, whereof one is so sore bruised, that it is feared he will not escape with his life.[68]

Starr was a neighbour of the Digger Henry Bickerstaffe at Painshill, and their families had clashed before. A generation before, Starr's father had been involved in violent conflicts with Bickerstaffe's father over boundaries and rights of way on recently enclosed lands near the hill. In 1619 James Starr was attacked and knocked to the ground by Robert Bickerstaffe's servants, and the ten-year-old William Starr witnessed his father being viciously beaten. There may well have been a personal element to Starr's response to the Diggers, though Winstanley characterised him as someone who argued that the commons rightfully belonged to the poor. For Winstanley, of course, that meant the Diggers, but for Starr it presumably meant those local inhabitants who had established use rights there.[69]

In late June the Diggers' opponents tried a different approach, and on the 23rd an action for trespass was begun against Winstanley and nine of his companions in Kingston's court of record. The suit was on behalf of Francis Drake, an MP who had been secluded at Pride's Purge and who was the lessee of the manor of Walton. Drake was a Puritan, whose mother, Joan Drake, had famously taken to her room having convinced herself that she was eternally damned. Some of Englands' most renowned divines had been brought in to persuade her that she was wrong, and it was only when she lay on her death bed that she accepted that she was one of the elect.[70] Francis Drake's own strong religious views would become apparent in his contribution to parliamentary debates in December 1656, when MPs were deciding on what punishment was most suitable for the Quaker James Nayler, who had ridden into Bristol on a mule in what was taken as being in imitation of Christ. Drake insisted that Nayler was guilty of 'horrid blasphemy', and he suggested that he was 'worse than all the papists in the world, worse than possessed with the devil'. While some might 'wash their hands of Nayler's blood', Drake was, he admitted, keen 'to wash my hands of the guilt of giving less than death': 'let us consider the honour of God, and the obligation upon us to vindicate it'.[71] Drake was unlikely to have had much sympathy for Winstanley and his ideals.

The Diggers came before the court on 7 July, but because they insisted on pleading their own cause, and refused to fee a lawyer, they were deemed not to have made an appearance. This happened again on 14 and 21 July, and Winstanley delivered up a paper criticising the court's proceedings. The paper was left unread, and on 28 July the jury assessed damages against the defendants, including damages of £10 plus costs in the cases of Winstanley and Henry Bickerstaffe. Bickerstaffe was imprisoned, but released three days later at Drake's instigation; a writ of execution was issued against Winstanley on 11 August, and very soon bailiffs were making their way to his Cobham home.[72] Winstanley's response was to intensify his criticisms of the court, and to rail against its jury 'made up of rich Free-holders, and such as stand strongly for the Norman power' and its 'covetuous besotted, ignorant Attorney Mr Gilder'.[73] His account of the bailiffs' actions in seizing the cattle at his farmstead is among the most moving and vivid of his writings, and the narrative skilfully brings out the confusion and excitement of the lengthy tussle with the court's officers. Four cows, none of which actually belonged to Winstanley (they may have belonged to his parents-in-law), were taken from his home and driven away; he was absent at the time, and found out what had happened only when 'some of the Lords Tenants rode to the next Town shouting the diggers were conquered, the diggers were conquered'. 'They took away the Cowes', he wrote, 'which were my livelihood',

> and beat them with their clubs, that the Cowes heads and sides did swell, which grieved tender hearts to see: and yet these Cowes never were upon *George* Hill, nor never digged upon that ground, and yet the poore beasts must suffer because they gave milk to feed me.

The cows were, however, quickly rescued by 'strangers'; they were 'driven out of those Devills hands the Bailiffes, and were delivered out of hell at that time'. Two weeks later the bailiffs returned and 'drove away seven Cowes and a Bull in the night time', some of them apparently belonging to a neighbour who had hired pasture from Winstanley. The gates around Winstanley's holding were opened, and 'Hogs and common Cattell' were allowed on to the barley and other crops growing there:

> So that the fury of this Norman Camp against the Diggers is so great, that they would not only drive away all the Cowes upon the ground, but spoyl the corn too, and when they had done this mischief, the Bayliffs, & the other Norman snapsack boyes went hollowing and shouting, as if they were dancing at a whitson Ale; so glad they are to do mischief to the Diggers, that they might hinder the work of freedome.[74]

Winstanley's lively account served to ridicule the Digger's opponents, with their cast made up of an 'old Norman Prerogative Lord' of the manor, the 'Norman theeves and pick-purses' of Kingston court, and the various 'sutlers', 'snapsack boyes, and ammunition drabs' all struggling to get a share of the spoils from Winstanley's poor, wizened cattle.[75] But it could not hide the fact that opposition to the Diggers, which had begun in April with unruly popular protests, was now much better organised. Along with the actions for trespass, there were meetings of local gentry and freeholders, and economic boycotts, with local people encouraged 'neither to buy or sell' with the Diggers. A landowner who had contracted to sell Winstanley three acres of grass was said to have sold it to someone else when the time came to mow; the Diggers' livelihoods away from St George's Hill were being effectively targeted. Winstanley's 'poor lean Cowes', which were 'little better the skin & bone' would, he noted, be poorer still in the winter 'for want of hay'. Surrey's ministers were active too in the campaign, supporting the boycott and establishing a lecture at Cobham 'to preach down the Diggers'.[76] The actions of the 'Norman Camp' were clearly taking their toll, for Henry Bickerstaffe appears to have left the digging at around this time. Within a short space of time Winstanley and his companions had retreated from the parish of Walton and had moved the site of their activities to the less hostile surroundings of Cobham. The occupation of St George's Hill had come to an end.

This reverse appears to have prompted Winstanley to rethink his tactics. His writings became more acerbic once again, closer in tone to *The True Levellers Standard*, and he was more openly critical of the slow pace of reform in the months following the execution of the king. In *A Watch-Word to the City of London*, the work in which he described his struggles with Kingston court, he grappled with the meaning of 'true freedom'. Many people had tried to define freedom, but few had any sense of what it was: 'you are all like men in a mist, seeking for freedom, and know not where, nor what it is'. For Winstanley it could exist only where the poor enjoyed free access to the commons. Freedom, Winstanley concluded, 'comes clothed in a clownish garment': he 'is the man that will turn the world upside downe, therefore no wonder he hath enemies'.[77] Winstanley also began to reflect more upon the concept of kingly power. In his *A New-Yeers Gift for the Parliament and Armie*, which was published at the end of the year, he explored the meanings of kingly power in detail, describing it as being 'like a great spread tree', for 'if you lop the head or top-bow, and let the other Branches and root stand, it will grow again and recover fresher strength'. The 'top-bow is lopped off the tree of Tyrannie', but 'oppression is a great tree still, and keeps off the sun of freedome from the poor Commons still, he hath many branches and great roots which must be grub'd up, before every one can sing Sions songs in peace'.[78]

In his Digger writings of the autumn and winter of 1649, Winstanley began to focus once more on the religious context of the digging, and on the raging battles between lamb and dragon and light and darkness. The apocalyptic message of *The New Law of Righteousnes* and *The True Levellers Standard* was forcefully reiterated in *A New-Yeers Gift* and in the later *Fire in the Bush*, a work that was both deeply religious and avowedly communist; this was also the period in which his early tracts were republished as *Several Pieces Gathered into one Volume.*[79] Winstanley's attitude towards landowners also became noticeably more confrontational from the autumn onwards. Although he continued to advance persuasive arguments from necessity, and sought to portray the digging as a useful means of enabling the poor to feed themselves, his earlier, carefully worded statements about not encroaching beyond the commons were fading from view. Instead, in the months that followed, we find much more belligerent statements, and claims that copyhold tenants as well as labourers should free themselves from the clutches of manorial lords.

The change in emphasis reflected in part the changed circumstances that the Diggers faced in Cobham. Many of the Diggers were now on home territory, and the local response to them was very different from what they had faced on St George's Hill. We certainly do not see a repeat in Cobham of the mass crowd actions of April, May and June. When attempts were made to evict them from their new encampment, the initiative came largely from local gentry rather than local yeomen and freeholders of the sort who had led the protests in Walton. Local hostility towards the Diggers seems to have been much more muted in Cobham than in Walton. Their leading local opponent was now John Platt, the West Horsley minister who held the manor of Cobham by right of his wife, and he was joined in his campaign by other Cobham gentlemen and by Sir Anthony Vincent, the powerful lord of the neighbouring manor of Stoke d'Abernon. When violence resumed the work was carried out largely – as Winstanley was quick to point out – by the tenants of Platt and Vincent and by men hired by them for the purpose.[80] The Diggers settled on Cobham's Little Heath, which was part of a large tract of common land in the eastern half of the parish, and appear to have been left unmolested for some time. It was not until October that the Council of State received information of 'tumultuous and riotous' gatherings around Cobham. Fairfax was again asked to send horse to Cobham to assist local Justices of the Peace in 'disperseing those riotours' and preventing their return.[81] Actions against the Diggers were continued in Kingston's court of record, and a number of Diggers were indicted at the Surrey quarter sessions; five were imprisoned for just over a month in the White Lion prison in Southwark.[82]

To make the Earth a common treasury. Slipware plate by Prue Cooper, 1994. Credit: John Gurney.

One major new problem facing Winstanley and his companions was John Platt's skill as an opponent. Platt was well connected, he was a political ally of several of Surrey's leading parliamentarians, and like Winstanley he appreciated the importance of establishing personal contact with Fairfax. In December Winstanley wrote in some frustration about Platt having lain 'almost a fortnight waiting and tempting the Lord Fairfax to send Souldiers to drive off the Diggers', and the lord general's mind was clearly swayed by reports that the Diggers were cavaliers, drunkards and 'a riotous people'. In vain Winstanley tried to persuade Fairfax that many of those who called on him to act were themselves royalists and had been active in the 1648 risings – which in the case of Sir Anthony Vincent's eldest son was certainly true.[83] In late November soldiers from Fairfax's regiment were present when two Digger houses were pulled down, in one case turning 'a poor old man and his wife out of doors to lie in the field in a cold night'. In *A New-Yeers Gift* Winstanley vividly described the scene, with Platt and Vincent sitting 'among the souldiers on horsback and coach'; they 'commanded their fearfull tenants to pull down one of the Diggers houses before their faces, and rejoyced with shouting at the fall'. The local inhabitants who carried out the work were, Winstanley maintained, 'poor enforced slaves'; they 'durst do no other, because their Land-lords and Lords looked on, for fear that they should be turned out of service, or their livings'.[84] Winstanley was also quick to point to the differences of opinion among the soldiers who were present when the attacks took place. Two soldiers were in attendance when a second house was pulled down, and one of them was said by Winstanley to have been 'very civill', while the other 'railed bitterly' and forced 'three Country-men to help him pull down the house'. Again, therefore, Winstanley was able to emphasise the lack of enthusiasm that Cobham's inhabitants had for this work: 'the men were unwilling to pull it down; but for fear of their Land-lords, and the threatning souldier, they did put their hands to pull it down'.[85] Not long before, 'a poor honest man' had, Winstanley claimed, been turned out of his house 'because he looked with a cheerfull countenance upon the Diggers':

Can the Turkish Bashaws hold their slaves in more bondage than these Gospel-professing Lords of Manors do their poor tenants? and is this not the kingly power? O You Rulers of *England*, I pray see that your own acts be obeyed, and let the oppressed go free.[86]

Winstanley tried to maintain a determined and optimistic tone in *A New-Yeers Gift*. Despite losing their houses, the Diggers were still 'mighty cheerfull, and their spirits resolve to wait upon God, to see what he will do', and they have built them some few little hutches like calf-cribs, and there they lie anights, and follow their work adayes still with wonderfull joy of heart, taking the spoyling of their goods cheerfully ... And they have planted divers Acres of Wheat and Rye, which is come up, and promises a very hopefull crop, committing their cause to God, and wait upon him, saying, O thou King of righteousnesse, do thine own work.[87]

The land, Winstanley again insisted, was 'made for all, and true religion is, To let every one enjoy it'. Change was inevitable, and 'the great Leveller, Christ our King of righteousness in us', would make everyone 'delight to let each other enjoy the pleasures of the earth, and shall hold each other no more in bondage'. He pitied the Diggers's opponents 'for the torment your spirit must go through', but he assured them that they too were 'part of the creation who must be restored'. It was a brave response, but difficult to sustain in the face of such powerful opposition. The one thing that would make the Diggers slacken in their work was, Winstanley acknowledged, 'want of Food, which is not much now, they being all poor People, and having suffered so much in one expence or other since they began': poverty was 'their greatest burthen; and if any thing do break them from the Work, it will be that'. Towards the end of *A New-Yeers Gift* he wrote movingly in what must have been intended as a valedictory passage:

And here I end, having put my Arm as far as my strength will go to advance Righteousness: I have Writ, I have Acted, I have Peace: and now I must wait to see the Spirit do his own work in the hearts of others, and whether *England* shall be the first Land, or some other, wherein Truth shall sit down in triumph.[88]

Winstanley's fears for the future of the Digger experiment may have been influenced by the changing attitude of the army, and particularly of senior officers, towards the Diggers. Although he appreciated that the decision to send soldiers to Cobham was taken in accordance with the Council's request for assistance, and acknowledged that most of the soldiers 'did not meddle ... but expressed sorrow to see the Passages', he felt that the

'General grant and the Soulders presence was a great crush to our business'.[89] Winstanley had spoken to Fairfax in the gallery at Whitehall on 12 December, and appears to have sensed a lack of sympathy for the Diggers among the officers present. One colonel supposedly told Winstanley that the Diggers were aiming to 'draw a company of People into Arms'; others among the 'great Officers' complained that the Diggers were infringing property rights by digging upon the commons. The officers' behaviour towards a 'poor Cavalier Gentlewoman' who tried to present a paper to Fairfax – 'a brisk little man and two or three more Colonels puld back the Paper' and laughed at the woman – seems to have confirmed Winstanley's suspicion that kingly power was as strong in the army as elsewhere.[90]

Tensions between the army and the Diggers had some connection with their competing claims for crown and common land. In July 1649, when the Diggers were still on St George's Hill, parliament had passed its act for the sale of crown lands, in a move designed to help settle the army's massive pay arrears. Sales of bishops', and dean-and-chapter lands – which included the manor of Ham, to which the King family's copyhold lands belonged – were already taking place. Soldiers were issued with debentures, which could be used for purchasing parts of the late king's estates, but the purchasers were often senior officers who had bought up their soldiers' debentures. When Fairfax came to St George's Hill, Winstanley justified the Diggers' occupation of the hill by stating that the land they had settled on was crown land.[91] In *A New-Yeers Gift* Winstanley was more explicit, and for the first time in print he extended the Digger claims to common land to crown, forest, dean-and-chapter and bishops' lands. He demanded that army officers and parliament men should not force common soldiers 'by long delay of Payment to sell you their deer bought Debenters for a thing of naught, and then to go and buy our common Land, and crown Land, and other Land that is the spoil one of another, therewith'. The army had freed the earth 'from one intanglement of Kinglie power': would the officers, he asked, now entangle the earth 'more, and worse by another degree of Kinglie power?' The common people had contributed fully to the victory over the king: 'We that are the poor commons, that paid our Money, and gave you free Quarter, have as much Right in those crown Lands and Lands of the spoil as you'. It was 'our joynt purchased inheritance', and for officers to 'take it to your selves, and turn us out, and buy and sell it among your selves' would be 'a cheat of the Kinglie swordlie power which you hold up'. Winstanley clearly suspected self-interest in those officers who 'begin to say you are not satisfied in your consciences to let us have' use of crown and common lands.[92]

A New-Yeers Gift was not, however, the Diggers' last publication, and the Cobham colony would continue for more than three months after Winstanley had apparently acknowledged that the venture was close to an end. It is possible that the request to Fairfax to 'continue your former kindnesse' had some effect, but what is most likely to have strengthened the Diggers' resolve was the visible support that their venture was beginning to gain across a wide area of southern England and the midlands.[93] By early 1650 new Digger colonies had been established at Wellingborough in Northamptonshire, Iver in Buckinghamshire and 'Cox Hall in Kent'. In May 1650 the Iver Diggers were claiming that digging was also taking place in Gloucestershire and Nottinghamshire, and possibly elsewhere in Buckinghamshire; they also claimed that there were Digger activities at Barnet, Enfield, Dunstable and 'Bosworth old in Northamptonshire'. At least two of these new Digger groups issued their own manifestos, and we know from the lists of signatories that most of those involved were – like so many of the Surrey Diggers – local inhabitants.[94] New recruits were also joining the Cobham Digger colony, some from Cobham and the surrounding area and others from further afield. The latter included Robert Coster, a talented writer whose powerfully written A Mite Cast Into the Common Treasury appeared in December 1649. Coster may also have cooperated with Winstanley in producing The Diggers Mirth, a verse work containing a Digger song and a Digger 'Christmass-Caroll'.[95]

Winstanley's Digger writings were also coming to have an influence over a wide range of heterodox figures. One activist who almost certainly read Winstanley, and absorbed some of his most important ideas, was George Foster, author of *The Sounding of the Last Trumpet* (1650). Another was the Abiezer Coppe, whose 'Ranter' writings show the influence of Winstanley, but who made clear the fact that he was not advocating 'digging-levelling'. Laurence Clarkson, the libidinous self-proclaimed 'Captain of the Rant' (who by his own admission threw himself readily into the excesses which disapproving contemporaries always associated with Ranterism), also appears to have come into contact with Winstanley and the Diggers; he may even have spent some time digging on the commons. If so, this may explain Winstanley's increasing hostility to 'the Ranting crew' and his warnings to fellow Diggers to steer clear of 'Lust of the flesh' and 'the practise of Ranting'. There are passages in his *Fire in the Bush* where he seems also to be addressing Clarkson's theological arguments directly. Clarkson later (in his Muggletonian phase) had harsh things to say about Winstanley.[96] Outside radical circles we also find Marchamont Nedham and the learned Anthony Ascham engaging with Winstanley's arguments.[97]

Among Baptists Digger ideas were also beginning to have an appreciable, and apparently disruptive impact. At the general Baptist churches at Fenstanton and Warboys in Huntingdon-shire, which had been established by Henry Denne in 1644, a number of church members appear to have fallen away in the period 1649–50. The Warboys church records mention the activities of the Diggers, Ranters and Levellers and Winstanley's prophecy that 'Israel must go free, and how the Lord would destroy all those that oppose the work of making the earth a common treasury'. The entry for the year 1650 states tersely that 'now began the churches too much to listen to the errors of the times, viz: of certain people called Diggers, Levellers and Ranters'. Some among the 'children of God' were tempted by 'those strange errors, insomuch that several churches were so shaken up that most of our Christian assemblies were neglected or broken up'. It seems clear from this passage that the problem was considered to be a general one among the Baptist churches, and not confined to Fenstanton or Warboys. It was not until 1651 that there began 'again to be some returning to the Lord', and 1653 when 'the church begins to flourish again'.[98]

Winstanley's possible influence over the early Quakers has attracted much attention over the years, but there has been little agreement as to its nature or extent. In the later seventeenth century a number of prominent clergymen, including Thomas Comber and the future Archbishop of Canterbury Thomas Tenison, saw Winstanley as the true originator of the principles of Quakerism, and in the first decade of the twentieth century Lewis Berens suggested that the similarities between Winstanley's ideas and those of the Quakers were too great to be wholly coincidental.[99] The argument that the early Quakers learnt from Winstanley was, in 1943, developed further in an important article by Winthrop S. Hudson.[100] Quaker historians were however much more sceptical: William Braithwaite, for instance, while noting the similarities between the ideas of Winstanley and George Fox, felt that the Digger and the founder of Quakerism were most likely to be 'independent products of the peculiar social and spiritual climate of the age'.[101] Scholars of the left, many of whom were reluctant to acknowledge that Winstanley died a Quaker, often tended to agree with Braithwaite.[102] There is however a tantalising reference to Winstanley, which has never been fully explained, in the works of Nathaniel Stephens, who was minister of the Leicestershire parish of Fenny Drayton in the 1640s when the young George Fox and his family were parishioners there. Stephens features in Fox's autobiographical *Journal* as a figure who took an interest in the young Fox, reportedly telling an acquaintance that 'there was never such a plant bred in England'; he soon suspected Fox of 'going after new lights', and before long he had become a spirited and determined opponent of his. Fox encountered Stephens several times after he left Drayton, for his family continued to live in Drayton and remained close to their minister, and he and Stephens clashed publicly in 1649 and again in 1655.[103]

The reference to Winstanley comes in Stephens's *A Plain and Easie Calculation of the Name, Mark and Number of the Name of the Beast* (1656), a work not often read except by those with an interest in seventeenth-century millenarianism. It is usually assumed that the work shows that Winstanley disputed with Stephens, but this widely held view seems to be based on a misreading of the text by Alexander Gordon, who in the late-nineteenth century wrote Stephens's entry for the *Dictionary of National Biography*.[104] In fact what Stephens has to say is much more interesting. In a passage addressing those 'who amongst us have departed from Ordinances, and from Scriptures, and are now for extraordinary Revelations', he warns them to consider whether they 'may not be deluded by the power of Satan'. Referring to people of his own acquaintance, he speaks of 'friends of my familiarity heretofore, whom I did conceive to be people of good hope' but who 'have departed first from the Ministery, and then have come to slight the Written Word; and then last of all, to hang upon Revelations, and extraordinary Enthusiasms of the Spirit'. Stephens goes on to claim that 'I have seen a Book scattered abroad by these men, it beareth the Title of *Gerard Winstanley his new Law of Righteousness*', a work that Stephens recognises as being significant not only for advocating community, but also for rejecting all outward forms. Although Stephens claims not to be talking of Quakers here (for 'what they are, and who they are, God knows'), he acknowledges that he *is* thinking of those who 'have so often in their mouths the *Whore of Babylon*, and, *Come out of Babylon my people*; and that every thing is Antichristian' – phrases and sentiments that were commonly associated with Quakers in the 1650s.[105] Unless Stephens was a particularly poor judge of character, and took on several protégés who ended up disappointing him, it is difficult not to wonder whether he had his old acquaintance George Fox in mind when writing this passage. At the very least it suggests that some in the radical milieu from which Fox emerged were aware of Winstanley's writings and inspired by them, and were keen to spread his message.

This should not be wholly surprising, for the early Quakers were certainly more directly involved in radical social agitation, and were more fiercely and openly critical of the status quo, than their brethren in later years. Fox's own early writings, with their apocalyptic tone, their criticism of corrupt forms of buying and selling and their identification with 'such Levellers that levels down the corruption and the filth', clearly bear this out.[106] The Quakers, as the leading revolutionary movement of the 1650s, were at the forefront of agitation against tithes, and many early Quakers were, like many of the Diggers, originally from rural communities. Most would have had a similar understanding to the Diggers of the conflictual nature of rural social relations. Although they never openly advocated community, in the way that Winstanley did, some Quakers shared the common radical belief that commons and wastes properly belonged to the poor.[107] Fox, for one, was critical of those who 'gets the earth under their hands, Commons, Wastes and Forrests, and Fels, and Mores, and Mountaines, and lets it lye wast, and calls themselves Lords of it, and keeps it from the people, when so many are ready to starve and begg'.[108]

But if Winstanley's influence was felt by those who came to build the early Quaker movement, it is most likely to have been through his religious writings, with their emphasis on the inner light and the seed and their rejection of outward ordinances and book learning. The Quakers had a rich body of radical religious belief to draw on, but Winstanley was being published, and read, just at the point when Fox and his allies were beginning to formulate their ideas. There is much that Fox had in common with Winstanley, and it would be surprising if he did not encounter Winstanley's writings in 1649 or 1650 when, as Winstanley put it, the digging experiment was 'the talk of the whole land' and Digger camps were being set up in areas where Fox was active.[109] Fox was, however, like Winstanley, unwilling to openly acknowledge any direct influence from earlier thinkers, and his *Journal* was never likely to reveal more than hints that he knew Winstanley's writings.[110]

One way the Diggers' message was being spread was through the use of emissaries, who travelled from Cobham seeking support for the digging on the Little Heath. We know something about their activities from the text of a letter, written by Winstanley, which was found with four Surrey Diggers who were arrested at Wellingborough in April 1650. The Diggers had travelled through eight counties, passing through several carefully chosen towns and villages – including Warboys in Huntingdonshire – where they would have hoped to find a sympathetic reception. Winstanley's letter was designed to solicit financial assistance, for the Diggers were, he acknowledged, short of foodstuffs and corn. In explaining the purpose of the digging Winstanley chose to emphasise the social and practical benefits of establishing community on the commons, and he linked this explicitly to the establishment of freedom. The appeal for assistance was directed at those who were 'Friends to universall freedome', and who saw the digging and planting of the commons as 'the first springing up of freedome, to make the earth a common treasury that every one may enjoy food and rayment freely by his labour upon the earth, without paying rents or homage to any fellow creature of his own kind'; everyone would be thereby 'delivered from the tyranny of the conquering power; and so rise up out of that bondage to enjoy the benefit of his Creation'.[111] The Diggers had refined their aims since they first appeared on St George's Hill, and Winstanley's conception of freedom was closer now to that found in his final, post-Digger work, *The Law of Freedom in a Platform*, where true freedom would be defined very much in terms of free access to the land and the fruits of the earth, which could be guaranteed only through the removal of the restraining power of landlords. No other types of freedom would be possible without the prior establishment of this 'true *Foundation-Freedom*'.[112]

Winstanley's letter is also of interest for what it tells us about the state of the Cobham Digger colony in the spring of 1650. The previous summer's work had all been lost, 'yet through inward faithfullnesse to advance freedome they keep the field still'. Several acres of corn had been planted, and four houses built, 'and now this season time goes on digging, endeavouring to plant as much as they can'.[113] The colony's survival still depended on the Diggers' ability to attract financial support from sympathisers across the country, but the general tone of Winstanley's letter was optimistic. We can see this optimism also in Winstanley's confident expressions of support for the Engagement, the oath which the new government sought to impose on all adult males in 1650. The Engagement bound those who took it to be 'true and faithful to the Commonwealth of England, as it is now established, without a King or House of Lords', and this naturally created difficulties for many.[114] Consciences were eased by the arguments advanced by many of the contributors to the so-called 'Engagement Controversy'. These authors argued that allegiance to any government that provided its people with protection was always warranted, however distasteful the origins of that government or the particular form it took. It would therefore be perfectly lawful for royalists or Presbyterians, or any others who had no love for the new regime, to take the Engagement.[115] In his *Englands Spirit Unfoulded*, Winstanley produced a typically singular contribution to the debates, quite out of line with the arguments advanced by other writers. For Winstanley, the Engagement, along with parliament's recent acts abolishing the office of king and declaring England to be a commonwealth or free state, targeted kingly power and guaranteed the rights of all to have access to the common land 'and so to recruite themselves with a comfortable livelihood'. England would be restored to its 'Creation right, as it was before any Conquest by sword came in', and all would be 'freed from the slavery of the *Norman* Conquest' and 'protected from the Power of Lords of Mannours'.[116] When 94 of Cobham's male parishioners lined up in St Andrew's church to take the Engagement on 16 March, Winstanley and his fellow Diggers were at the front of the queue. John Coulton was the second parishioner to take the Engagement, Winstanley the third and Thomas Starr the fourth, while other Diggers followed further behind, mingling with their friends, relatives and even opponents.[117]

Optimism and self-confidence were apparent too in *An Appeale to all Englishmen*, which was dated 26 March. It was in this work that Winstanley and his fellow Diggers, building on the arguments advanced in *Englands Spirit Unfoulded*, announced that since the army and parliament had declared against 'all *Kingly* and *Lordly* entanglements', there were no longer any legal impediments to planting or building on the commons. Copyhold tenants were also now freed from obedience to their manorial lords and from paying customary dues to them or attending their manorial courts. All the old laws that upheld the rights of lords of manors were now cast out and abolished, and if tenants resisted the demands of their manorial lords, they would be protected by law. Tenants and labourers were urged not to

'enter into a new bond of slavery, now that you are come to the
point that you may be free, if you will stand up for freedom':
'nothing is wanting on your part, but courage and faithfulness'.
Advancing the work of freedom in the earth would free the
land of beggary and idleness, bring down food prices, reduce
crime, set an example to other nations and unite the English in
opposition to any foreign enemies. England would in a few years
become 'the richest, the strongest, and flourishing Land in the
World, and all *Englishmen* would live in peace and comfort'.
The rich themselves should willingly join in, and 'take Plow and
Spade, build and plant, and make the wast Land fruitfull'.[118]

There are even hints in Winstanley's writings that he hoped
that Parson Platt, the Diggers' inveterate enemy, might be
persuaded to leave them in peace. Winstanley continued to goad
the clergy in print, pointing out that 'they lay claime to Heaven
after they are dead, and yet they require their Heaven in this
World too'; the clergy told the poor that 'they must be content
with their poverty, and shall have their Heaven hereafter'. 'But
why', he asked them, 'may we not have our Heaven here, (that
is, a comfortable livelihood in the earth.) And Heaven hereafter
too, as well as you, *God is no respector of Persons*?' Platt was,
however, said by Winstanley to have used 'loving expressions,
and words savouring of much moderation, tenderness and
reason' in discussions with the Diggers, and he reportedly
offered to leave them alone if they stopped cutting wood on the
commons, an offer that the Diggers were prepared to accept. On
the other hand, Platt's further promise to throw in his lot with
the Diggers if they could prove that digging was warranted by
the scriptures, should perhaps have persuaded Winstanley not
to take his professions of friendship too seriously.[119]

By the beginning of April the Diggers' opponents were ready
to act. Fifteen Diggers, including Winstanley, were indicted
at the Southwark assizes for riots committed on St George's
Hill the previous year, and four were presented for the illegal
erection of cottages in Cobham.[120] Internal dissension may also
have begun to weaken the Digger cause. Winstanley's warnings
against 'the Ranting practise' and 'king lust of the flesh' became
more urgent in the spring of 1650, and he suspected that money

was being fraudulently collected by persons masquerading as Digger emissaries. Perhaps they had no connection with the digging, but it may be that they were Diggers who had fallen out with Winstanley.[121] It was however Platt and his associates who decided the fate of the Cobham Digger colony. Just before Easter Platt appeared with Thomas Sutton and several hired men and pulled down a 'poor mans house that was built upon the Commons': they 'kikt and struck the poor mans wife, so that she miscarried of her Child, and by the blowes and abuses they gave her, she kept her bed a week'.[122] On 19 April they appeared again, and on this occasion they had clearly decided to bring the digging venture to an end. Winstanley's eye-witness account is powerfully written, and reveals his great indignation at what happened. We can assume that it is trustworthy, since his text is corroborated in important respects by the surviving legal evidence.[123]

On this occasion Platt and his associates had decided to burn, rather than pull down the Diggers' houses, so as not to leave behind materials that could be reused:

> They set fire to six houses, and burned them down, and burned likewise some of their housholdstuffe, and wearing Clothes, throwing their beds, stooles, and housholdstuffe, up and down the Common, not pittying the cries of many little Children, and their frighted Mothers, which are Parishioners borne in the Parish.

When some Diggers returned that night they were threatened again, and told that their remaining possessions would be burnt if they did not leave:

> Thereupon Sir *Anthony Vincents* Servant, called *Davy*, struck at one, and cut some of their Chaires and other Goods to peeces, frightening the women and Children again. And some of the Diggers asked them, why they would do thus cruelly by them, they answered, because you do not know God, nor will not come to Church.

Men were hired to 'attend both night and day, to beat the Diggers, and to pull down their tents or houses, if they make any more'; and if the Diggers 'make Caves in the earth, they threaten to murther them there'. The Diggers' eleven acres of corn were abandoned and spoiled by cattle: 'Are not these men', Winstanley asked, 'the curse of *England*, that wil not suffer others to live by them, and will rather spoile corne in these dear times, then let the poor enjoy their own righteous labors upon the Commons?'[124]

For Winstanley, the fury of Parson Platt 'exceeds the fury of any other Lord of Mannor', and his actions confirmed in his mind the corruption of the church he represented. Winstanley concluded his account of the events of 19 April by contrasting the Diggers' 'patience, quietness, joy and sweet rest in their hearts' and the love they felt for their enemies, with their opponents' impatience and their 'fretting, jearing, rayling, and gnashing their tongues with vexation'. The Diggers' 'weak flesh' had been trodden down, but morally they were the victors:

> This work of digging, being freedom, or the appearance of Christ in the earth, hath tried the Priests and professors to the uttermost, and hath ripped up the bottom of their Religion, and proves it meere witchcraft, and cosonage; for self love and covetousnesse is their God, or ruling power. They have chosen the sword, and they refuse love; when the Lamb turnes into the Lion, they will remember what they have done, and mourne.[125]

Winstanley's work on the commons had lasted twelve-and-a-half months, but it was now at an end. The Diggers drifted away from Cobham, some of them – now deprived of their homes and work – leaving their children on the parish.[126] Some Surrey Diggers and Digger sympathisers continued the fight by trying to prosecute Platt, Thomas Sutton, William Starr, William Davey and several others for their part in burning the houses on the Little Heath, but the case was dismissed by the assize grand jury at Croydon in July 1650. The Iver Diggers were still active in May, but the Wellingborough Digger colony lasted only from March to April, when Thomas Pentlow, a Northamptonshire JP who would soon gain a reputation for persecuting Quakers, took action to suppress it.[127] Winstanley maintained that 'this righteous work of earthly community, shall have a most glorious resurrection' out of the ashes of kingly power; he also insisted that he remained

> assured of the righteousnesse of the work, and it shall take root in one place or other, before many yeares passe over *Englands* head, I can set no time, but I wait for the consolation of *Israel* to arise up, and break forth in others, as I have a taste of him in my self.[128]

But after the disappearance of the Wellingborough and Iver colonies, no more was to be heard of attempts to bring freedom through digging the commons. The vision that inspired Winstanley, and had attracted such promising levels of support, would survive only in a rather different form. Shorn of is central commitment to the establishment of community, it would resurface most powerfully in the rapidly growing Quaker movement of the 1650s. It is not surprising that as early as 1653 the minister Francis Higginson anticipated Tenison and Comber by claiming that the Quakers were drawing on 'the learning of Winstanley and Collier'.[129] Nor is it surprising that Winstanley sought out the first Quaker missionaries who reached London in 1654, and was said to have told them that they were 'sent to perfect that worke, which fell in their handes'.[130] But before this time Winstanley had the opportunity to reconsider his ideas in the light of recent experience, and to make a last, bold attempt to advocate the establishment of community. This was in his best-known publication, *The Law of Freedom in a Platform*.

4

A New Beginning?

Winstanley completed *The Law of Freedom in a Platform* in November 1651, and it appeared in print the following February. If Winstanley's account of its origins is correct, the work was written in several stages, and had been begun while the Diggers were still occupying the commons. He had, he claimed in November 1651, intended the work to see the light of day 'above two yeares ago, but the disorder of the Times caused me to lay it aside'; only recently had he been 'stirred up to give it a resurrection, and to pick together as many of my scattered papers as I could finde, and to compile them into this method'.[1] It is not surprising that Winstanley found little time to work on it in the final stages of the digging experiment, or in the months following the Diggers' expulsion from Cobham's Little Heath. The threat of legal proceedings hung over the Diggers for at least a year after they ended their activities, and Winstanley may have found it difficult during this period to return to his home in Cobham.[2] He was also busy for some months in 1650 on a new and unexpected venture, which was to end as abruptly as the digging.

It was in August 1650 that Winstanley and a number of his fellow Diggers came to stay at Pirton in Hertfordshire, where the high-born prophetess Lady Eleanor Douglas was owner of the Rectory manor. The manor had been bought for her as a jointure by her first husband, the poet and politician Sir John Davies, but it had later been lost to creditors; she had only recently regained possession after a lengthy series of legal actions. The Lady Eleanor, as she called herself, had a long and troubled history as a prophetic writer. Having become convinced of her mission in 1625, she had correctly predicted the deaths of her first husband and the Duke of Buckingham, and had become

a bitter enemy of Archbishop Laud. Both of her husbands had
tried to silence her by burning her manuscripts, and her second
husband, Sir Archibald Douglas, allowed much of her estate to
be dispersed. In 1631 she and her family failed in their attempts
to save the life of her brother, the notorious Earl of Castlehaven,
who was tried by his peers and executed for crimes of rape and
sodomy. Two years later she was fined £3,000 by the court of
High Commission and committed to prison for her writings. She
spent several years in prison and in Bethlem Hospital, the latter
committal coming after she had poured tar, or worse, over the
altar of Lichfield Cathedral. She welcomed the fall of Charles I,
and in December 1649 she produced – like Winstanley – a *New-
Years-Gift*. She believed that 1650 was to be a year of jubilee
and restitution.[3] It is likely that at least initially she welcomed
the fugitive Diggers into her home.

Winstanley was at Pirton from 20 August until December
1650. During this time he and his companions threshed at least
60 loads of wheat, cut wood and dug and prepared the garden
for the spring. He also succeeded – so he claimed – in saving the
year's crop by getting a sequestration taken off the estate.[4] It was
probably the stay at Pirton that gave rise, as Christopher Hill
suggested, to Laurence Clarkson's well-known comments about
Winstanley's 'most shameful retreat from *Georges-hill*, with a
spirit of pretended universality, to become a real Tithe-gatherer
of propriety'.[5] These comments have often seemed puzzling, and
it has sometimes been assumed that they indicate that Winstanley
himself quickly became an acquisitive property owner after the
failure of the digging venture. To A.L. Rowse, for instance, they
were proof that 'Winstanley was no better than the rest of the
Saints – out for his own ends'.[6] But the Pirton connection makes
much more sense. As holder of the Rectory manor, Lady Eleanor
was impropriator of the living at Pirton, and she was said in
1650 to be in receipt of 'all the tythes and profittes ariseinge in
the sayed parish'.[7] Much of her income from her Pirton estate
would have come from the tithes paid by the parishioners. The
corn threshed by the Diggers, and saved from sequestration by
Winstanley, was tithe corn. In working for Douglas at Pirton,
Winstanley was very openly involved in tithe gathering, an

occupation with which few radicals would have wanted to be
associated in 1650.

The Diggers' stay at Pirton was clearly a difficult one. It seems
that Winstanley feared that the Lady Eleanor saw him as little
more than an underling: 'I came not under your rooffe', he later
told her, 'to earne money like a slave ... you know I asked you
nothing'. When she visited Pirton, four of the threshers were
forced to wait on her for the best part of a week, and had to help
her coachmen dress the horses. On 3 December she travelled up
from London again and appeared unexpectedly in Pirton's tithe
barn. This was, Winstanley wrote, 'that remarkable day wherein
you came as the scriptures speakes like a theeff in the night, to
call me to judgment; before any forewarneing, to pick a hole
in my coat'. The Lady Eleanor, who had decided to assume the
guise of Melchizedeck the king of Salem, berated Winstanley
and apparently charged him with attempting to provide false
accounts. Winstanley responded the following day, in an
extraordinary letter that combines incredulity, pity and extreme
combativeness. Had she but asked to see his accounts he would
'freely have brought or sent them to you' and 'clered things in
moderacon'. Instead she had come as Melchizedeck, 'which is
a high assumption, you might as well call your self The christ,
for you sett your self in the chare of the Allmightie god'. She
was, he informed her, full of 'secrett prid, & self will'; 'the true
prophettes' were 'noe tax masters over their brethren, they did
worke with there owne hands, to eate bread, as well as to desire
others to worke with & for them'. A 'proud self willed spirit, that
will not be guided by reason, is the most low, base & ignoblest
spirit in the earth'; she would be chained 'up in darknes, till
Reason, which you have trampled under foott, come to set you
free'. The Lady Eleanor was, as he insisted on reminding her,
'noe more to me then any other branch of mankind'.[8]

It seems very unlikely that the Diggers remained at Pirton
much beyond 4 December. Winstanley's clash with his fellow
visionary was another unexpected reverse to add to the many
he had suffered over the previous year. The Winstanley who
emerged in *The Law of Freedom* was wiser and more cautious
than in his Digger writings, and clearly less optimistic about the

ease with which the power of the Beast could be overcome. *The Law of Freedom* differs from his earlier works in several respects, not least because it is the only one in which he attempted to provide a detailed description of the new society he hoped to see established. Property would be held in common, and buying and selling, the practice of law for money, and preaching for hire, would all be outlawed. Coin might be retained for trade with other nations, but gold and silver would in general be better used for making 'dishes and other necessaries for the ornament of houses'. Winstanley envisaged a network of common storehouses and public shops, which would hold wares and materials needed for manufacture and consumption, and from which goods could be freely withdrawn according to need:

> Every Tradesman shall fetch Materials, as Leather, Wool, Flax, Corn, and the like, from the publike Store-houses to work upon without buying and selling; and when particular works are made, as Cloth, Shooes, Hats, and the like, the Tradesmen shall bring these particular works to particular shops, as it is now in practise, without buying and selling. And every family as they want such things as they cannot make, they shall go to these shops, and fetch without money, even as now they fetch with money.[9]

The individual family lay at the heart of Winstanley's system. The earth would be 'planted, and the fruits reaped, and carried into Store-houses by common assistance of every Family', and the contents of storehouses would be 'the Common Stock to every Family'. Each family would however live apart from the rest of the community, and their household goods and furniture would remain their own. Winstanley was obviously still sensitive to the accusation that community of property went hand in hand with community of partners, and still mindful from his Digger days of the disruptive effects of the 'ranting' impulse. The head of the family, who Winstanley seems to have assumed would always be male, was one commonwealth's officer among many, and 'the first link of the chain Magistracy'. All offices were connected 'like links of a Chain', and all arose from 'the same root, which is necessity of Common Peace'.[10] Office holders would generally be drawn from those over 40, and they would be elected on an annual basis; no one would be permitted to hold office for more than a year at a time. The experience of office holding would thus be spread widely, at least among the nation's male inhabitants. Parliament, as 'Representative of the whole Land' and 'Head Power in a Commonwealth', would be empowered to remove grievances, abolish all old oppressive laws and customs, mobilise the nation in times of war and promote and oversee the 'free planting and reaping of the Commonwealths Land', which Winstanley now took to include former monastic lands as well as crown and bishops' lands, parks, forests, chases and commons and wastes. The chief role of a commonwealth's army would be to 'beat down all that arise to endeavor to destroy the Liberties of the Commonwealth': a commonwealth's army was, he suggested, like John the Baptist, who 'levels the Mountains to the Valleys, pulls down the Tyrant, and lifts up the Oppressed, and so makes way for the spirit of Peace and Freedom to come in to rule and inherit the Earth'.[11]

The role of ministers would be radically different from what had gone before. Ministers would like other officers be subject to annual election, and at weekly parish gatherings they would be responsible for passing on news and, on four times a year, for reading out (though not interpreting) the laws of the commonwealth. They would also talk of history, science and 'the Nature of Mankind', and people would come to know 'the secrets of Nature and Creation, within which all true knowledg is wrapped up'. It was a bold endorsement by Winstanley of experimental knowledge and another example of his rejection of 'imagination' and book learning. Winstanley was well aware that existing ministers would see this as but 'a low and carnal ministry', which 'leads men to know nothing, but the knowledge of the earth, and the secrets of nature'. But for Winstanley, 'to know the secrets of nature, is to know the works of God; And to know the works of God within the Creation, is to know God himself, for God dwels in every visible work or body'.[12]

Others besides the minister would also have freedom to speak at weekly parish meetings if they had anything useful to say: 'everyone who hath any experience, and is able to speak of any Art or Language, or of the Nature of the Heavens above, or of the Earth below, shall have free liberty to speak when they offer themselves'. Speeches might be made in English or in a foreign language,

> so that men of our English Commonwealth may attain to all Knowledges, Arts and Languages, and that every one may be encouraged in his Industry, and purchase the countenance and love of their neighborhood, for their wisdom, and experimental knowledge in the things which are.

All children would receive an education, though none would be permitted to be 'trained up onely to book learning, and no other employment'. Marriage would be openly entered into, for 'every man and woman shall have the free liberty to marry whom they love' without any hindrance of birth or marriage portion. The marriage ceremony would consist of a simple declaration by both parties, made in the presence of neighbours and overseers.[13]

Running through the work were Winstanley's thoughts on the nature of freedom, law and the origins of magistracy. Winstanley acknowledged, as he had done in his Digger writings, that 'the great searching of heart in these days, is to finde out where true Freedom lies, that the Commonwealth of *England* might be established in peace'. Much of what was commonly defined as freedom he rejected. True freedom for Winstanley lay in the free enjoyment of the earth; without this, no other types of freedom were possible. The fundamental law governing society was the law of necessity, and the original root and 'Foundation-Rule' of magistracy was common preservation. Government was of two kinds, kingly and commonwealth's; the first grew out of covetousness and self-preservation, the second out of common preservation, concern for others and the desire for unity, peace and freedom. Winstanley aimed at the establishment of 'true *Foundation-Freedom* which settles a Commonwealth in Peace'. Because of the varied nature of humankind – 'some are wise, some are foolish, some idle, some laborious, some rash, some milde, some loving and free to others, some envyous and covetous' – laws were necessary for the preservation of the common peace. There must, he insisted, 'be suitable Laws for every occasion, and almost for every action that men do'; there must also be fit officers, and a faithful execution of the law. Together these would provide 'the Foundation and Pillars of Commonwealths Government'.[14]

The Law of Freedom was little known before the 1890s, but the Marxists who encountered it then were quick to recognise it as a classic of socialist literature. Eduard Bernstein, for instance, devoted a whole chapter in his contribution to Kautsky's *Forerunners* to Winstanley's 'communist utopia', a work that for him dropped all paraphrase and could be seen to provide a realistic and perceptive description of a complete framework for a socialist social order.[15] It was almost certainly this work, rather than the visions and activities of the Diggers, which guaranteed Winstanley a place on the Alexander Gardens monument in Moscow.

And yet *The Law of Freedom* has often seemed troubling, and less an advance on his earlier positions than a retreat from the optimistic belief in human perfectibility that permeated *The New Law of Righteousnes*. One striking feature is the patriarchal nature of Winstanley's vision, with its focus on the nuclear family unit invariably headed by a male. In *The New Law of Righteousnes* Winstanley had written confidently of Christ rising in both sons and daughters. His use in *The True Levellers Standard* of the words 'every single Man, Male, and Female' may sound curious to modern ears, but suggests a sensitivity to gender unusual among male writers of the seventeenth century.[16] In *The Law of Freedom* the role in society of women and girls was, however, to be a clearly subordinate one: the education of girls would be different from that enjoyed by boys, while adult women would apparently play no part in government and have no independent control over their household.[17] Winstanley's proposal to transfer women and children to other households in the absence of a capable male head was, as Ann Hughes has noted, much more limiting than existing practice, which allowed for widows and singlewomen to act as heads of households.[18] While Hughes has emphasised Winstanley's 'basic adherence to patriarchal authority', Phyllis Mack has concluded that Winstanley's social philosophy, though 'radical in terms of class relationships, is conservative to the core in terms of gender'.[19]

Also striking is Winstanley's emphasis on the need for laws 'for every occasion and almost for every action that men do'. A substantial part of *The Law of Freedom* was taken up with detailed descriptions of the offices, laws and punishments required under commonwealth's government.[20] There were to be at least 13 categories of state officer, and 62 'particular Laws ... whereby a Commonwealth may be governed'. Punishments for the infringement of laws would include temporary servitude 'for such as have lost their freedom' and the death penalty, while in every town, city or parish one of the elected officers would be the executioner, who was empowered to 'cut off the head, hang, or shoot to death, or whip the offender according to the sentence of Law'.[21] All this seems a far cry from Winstanley's earlier writings, with their denunciation of 'imprisoning, whiping and killing' as 'but the actings of the curse'.[22] While some on the left have seen the shift in Winstanley's position as a realistic one, reflecting the realisation that even after victory 'the state and the army may be necessary as instruments in the hands of the redeemed against the unredeemed',[23] anarchist and left-libertarian writers have often been less charitable. Marie-Louise Berneri, for example, thought that *The Law of Freedom* revealed 'an authoritarian spirit common to most utopians', and that in this work Winstanley's 'conception of justice was wholly barbaric'. More recently Peter Marshall has portrayed *The Law of Freedom* as a work that offered 'a new and authoritarian version of communist society', and that showed clearly how 'Winstanley's libertarian genius had left him after his exhausting experience of practical communism'.[24]

There are many other ways in which Winstanley can appear more hard headed, and less idealistic, in *The Law of Freedom* than in his earlier writings. In *Fire in the Bush* there is the moving passage where he speaks of the innocence of youth: 'Looke upon a childe that is new borne, or till he growes up to some yeares, he is innocent, harmelesse, humble, patient, gentle, easie to be entreated, not envious.' In *The Law of Freedom*, by contrast, 'Mankinde in the days of his youth, is like a young Colt, wanton and foolish, till he be broke by Education and correction.'[25] A passage that impressed the first Marxist readers of *The Law of Freedom* was the one – still frequently cited – in which Winstanley proclaimed his assurance 'that if it be rightly searched into, the inward bondages of mind, as covetousness, pride, hypocrisy, envy, sorrow, fears, desperation, and madness, are all occasioned by the outward bondage, that one sort of people lay upon another'. This passage, more than any other, could for some readers be taken to demonstrate a clear shift in Winstanley's thinking from a position of chiliastic mysticism to the adoption of a fully fledged materialist analysis of society.[26]

It is important not to overstate the differences between *The Law of Freedom* and Winstanley's earlier writings. There are hints in Winstanley's earlier works that the system of law and government set out in *The Law of Freedom* did not necessarily represent a major change of principle. As has already been noted, Winstanley had acknowledged in *The New Law of Righteousnes* the possibility of disobedience and recalcitrance in the new society, and had allowed for the temporary loss of freedom for those who broke the law of righteousness or who 'steal or whore or become idle and wil not work'.[27] In his Digger writings Winstanley was also always insistent that he was not against law or government: 'True Government', he wrote, 'is that I long for to see'.[28] There are hints too of patriarchalism in the Digger writings, not least in the total absence of the names of women from Digger manifestos. We know nothing at all of Susan Winstanley from her husband's writings, despite the occasional references in them to his own experiences. Was she persuaded by his ideas, and did she join him in his digging venture? We simply do not know, since Winstanley has left us no record of her.

The millenarianism that informed his earlier works was also still evident in *The Law of Freedom*. Winstanley's hopes were still pinned on the 'spirit of universal Righteousness dwelling in Mankinde, now rising up to teach every one to do to another as he would have another do to him', which was the 'great Lawgiver in Commonwealths Government'.[29] Kingly government was the 'great Antichrist, and Mystery of Iniquity', and must pass away. *The Law of Freedom* was dedicated to Oliver Cromwell, who as the commander of the army was the most powerful individual in the commonwealth in 1651, and it has often been thought that this demonstrated Winstanley's conversion to the belief that state action, rather than Christ rising, was what was now required to bring about the new society. As Winstanley informed Cromwell in his dedicatory epistle, 'you have power in your hand ... to Act for Common Freedome if you will; I have no power'. Yet there is no indication that he hoped of any more from Cromwell than assistance in advancing commonwealth's government by using his power to make available commons, wastes, and other commonwealth's lands for the use of the poor. Winstanley also reminded Cromwell that the 'spirit of the whole creation (who is God) is about the Reformation of the World, and he will go forward in his work'; and 'if he will not spare Kings, who have sat so long at his right hand, governing the World, neither will he regard you, unless your ways be found more righteous then the Kings'. Change was, it seems, still bound to come, with or without Cromwell's help.[30]

It is also important to bear in mind the context in which *The Law of Freedom*, at least in its finished version, was produced. Thomas Hobbes's *Leviathan* had appeared in the spring of 1651, and Winstanley may well, as some scholars have suggested, have been keen to engage with the Hobbesian arguments that were making headway at the time he was writing *The Law of Freedom*.[31] Perhaps more significant was the fact that the current of radical argument had shifted significantly since the days of digging, and radical hopes were now increasingly channelled towards the cause of structured legal, religious and constitutional reform.[32] The emphasis on laws, fit officers and the proper execution of the law was to be found in the work of many radical propagandists in 1651, among them Hugh Peter and the future Quaker Isaac Penington junior – whose work Winstanley had almost certainly read when he wrote *The Law of Freedom*.[33]

The shift in emphasis was in part a reflection of the radical split of 1649. While many radicals, particularly those associated with gathered churches, quickly became firm supporters of the new regime, the Levellers, as we have seen, denounced the political changes of 1648–49 as a betrayal of radical hopes and the nation's interests. For godly supporters of the republic, what mattered most was that virtuous individuals – those who would always put the public good above their own self-interest – should be in control of the machinery of government. They could be trusted to advance the public interest, and were constrained by what the Levellers saw as fundamental laws only to the extent, as John Canne put it, that 'they see the same conducing to the welfare and happinesse of the Republick'; they could 'lay aside either part or whole (as they see cause) and appoint something else more seasonable and proper to us, and as providence makes way for it'.[34] The Levellers, by contrast, appreciated that even the most virtuous individuals could be corrupted by office, particularly when their actions were not limited by generally recognised constitutional constraints. It was primarily for this reason that they called for a written constitutional agreement to which all consented, and which set out clearly those fundamentals that no government could alter.[35] The Levellers' insistence on the need for government based on laws rather than men was of course famously taken up by James Harrington, whose 1656 work *The Commonwealth of Oceana* provided a detailed model of a system of government based on precisely this principle. Like the Levellers, but unlike the godly, Harrington would also see no need to radically restrict participation in elections and office holding, since all alike were inclined to corruption.

The implications of the divisions between the Levellers and their former allies would not necessarily have been evident to Winstanley when he embarked upon the occupation of St George's Hill, but it seems certain that they influenced his thinking in 1651. For Winstanley, it was clear that good laws were necessary to hold errant behaviour in check, and it was equally important for those laws to be widely known and understood. Hence the obligation on ministers to regularly read out the laws, and for laws to be 'few, short and pithy'. If all were familiar with the laws they would be less likely to break them, and less likely to suffer the penalties imposed for their infringement. Winstanley also recognised the value of broad participation both in elections and government, and he was, by contemporary standards, generous when it came to deciding the categories of those who might be allowed to participate in elections or to hold office. His advocacy of frequent elections and rotation of office clearly demonstrated his acceptance of the argument that office holding should be widely spread, and that long tenure of office tended to corruption. 'Great Offices in a Land and Army' have, he pointed out, 'changed the disposition of many sweet spirited men', and like Lilburne before him he made use of the proverb 'if water stand long, it corrupts'. No Leveller would have disagreed with his observation that

> When publique Officers remain long in place of Judicature, they will degenerate from the bounds of humility, honesty, and tender care of brethren, in regard the heart of man is so subject to be overspred with the clouds of covetousness, pride, and vain-glory: for though at the first entrance into places of Rule they be of publique spirits, seeking the Freedom of others as their own; yet continuing long in such a place, where honors and greatness is coming in, they become selfish, seeking themselves, and not common Freedom; as experience proves it true in these days.[36]

Much of what seems surprising to us in *The Law of Freedom* when compared with Winstanley's earlier writings would, it seems, have appeared intelligible and quite familiar to a radical readership in 1651 and 1652. A great many writers were seeking to contribute to debates on reform in the period following Cromwell's victory at Worcester in September 1651; Winstanley's was one voice among many. His essential aim – which was to advance community – remained the same as before, but in *The Law of Freedom* he chose to express it in ways that reflected the current preoccupations of radical thinkers and writers. It was a bold attempt to repeat his earlier arguments in a form more appropriate to the times, but it seems unlikely that many readers would have been persuaded by his case for establishing community. For the majority of participants in the reform debates of the early 1650s, the need to advance commerce and create wealth, and to build up a commercially minded republic to rival the Dutch, was what mattered most; arguments in favour of community may have belonged more to the heady days of 1649 than to the present.[37]

Some of Winstanley's arguments clearly had an impact, even
if the readers who encountered them were largely unaware of
his advocacy of communism. In 1652 several highly selective
extracts from *The Law of Freedom* appeared anonymously in
newsbooks and other publications.[38] None of these extracts
hinted at Winstanley's core message, but they provided readers
with robust criticisms of the failings of governments and armies,
and arguments in favour of the reform of the law.[39] Whether
Winstanley had a hand in this is unclear. It would certainly have
been an effective way of reaching new readers, and Winstanley
did acknowledge in *The Law of Freedom* that his 'Platform of
Government' contained useful things even for those who could
never be persuaded to do away with buying and selling.[40] Similar
selections had been made of some of Winstanley's Digger writings
in 1649, which suggests that he may always have been willing to
allow watered-down versions of his arguments to appear if this
enabled him to reach a wider audience.[41] One person who would
not normally have been expected to read Winstanley's writings,
but who unwittingly endorsed arguments from *The Law of
Freedom*, was none other than Oliver Cromwell. In April 1652
he was handed a set of anonymous propositions for 'the better
regulating of the Law', which incorporated extracts from *The
Law of Freedom*. Cromwell is said to have 'seriously weighed and
considered' these propositions and to have declared his strong
support for regulating the law. This may have been as close the
work's dedicatee ever got to reading *The Law of Freedom*.[42]

The Law of Freedom was the last of Winstanley's publications,
and his later thoughts on social, political and religious questions
are lost to us. For the period from 1652 until 1676, the year of
Winstanley's death, we are reliant chiefly upon legal documents
and probate, church and quarter sessions records for tracing the
outlines of his life. The available sources are patchy, and in some
cases open to multiple interpretations. We have to be cautious
about how they are used, and must always be aware that they
can only ever provide us with a partial understanding of how
he responded to the major political and religious developments
of his later years.[43] What we do know is that Winstanley had
returned to Cobham by June 1652, for on the 15th of that

month he was a witness to the will of his friend John Coulton, in the company of two other Cobham residents who had had no involvement in the digging.[44] Two years later he made contact, as we have seen, with Edward Burrough and other Quakers when they made their first appearance in London. His words of encouragement did not mean that he was ready yet to throw in his lot with this vibrant new movement, and it was to be some years before he definitely became a Quaker.[45] His return to Cobham brought him back to a life of farming, and in 1658 we see him engaging in manorial land transactions in the manor of Ham. In 1659 he was elected parish waywarden in Cobham, and in the following year overseer of the poor. He must have conformed to the Church of England after the restoration of monarchy, for in 1667–8 and 1668–9 he served as churchwarden for Cobham. Winstanley also served as a juror at quarter sessions, and in October 1671 he was appointed one of the two high constables for Elmbridge hundred, a position of some responsibility in the county.[46]

St Andrew's Church, Cobham. Winstanley was churchwarden here 1667–69. Credit: John Gurney.

We cannot be sure of the significance of these developments. It seems unlikely, given what we know of his earlier attitudes to organised religion, that he would suddenly have felt any strong affinity for the restored Church of England. Even in his Digger days he had spoken approvingly of parochial office, and his assumption of the roles of waywarden, overseer and churchwarden in Cobham may have reflected a sense of civic duty as much as anything else. The Quaker Ephraim Carter served as an overseer of the poor for Cobham in 1664–5, and elsewhere Quakers, familists and other dissenters are known to have taken on local office (though rarely the office of churchwarden) and to have been willing to play their part in the local community.[47] Certainly Winstanley seems to have been unusually conscientious as churchwarden in distributing parochial charities to the local poor, including former Diggers, and in chasing up charities that had been diverted to other uses. In both his years as churchwarden he spent more money than he received.[48] His willingness to conform, at least outwardly, to the restored Church of England may even indicate that his views of organised religion had not changed significantly since 1651. If his hostility to all existing churches remained undimmed, it may have been easier for him to go through the motions of attending his parish church, as required by law, than it would have been for nonconformists who had alternative churches and forms of worship to turn to. Those whose consciences led them to identify strongly with forms proscribed by the restored church were perhaps less likely to conform than those who identified with none. If he was as yet unconvinced by the Quakers, where exactly could Winstanley turn after 1660?

But when we look at the careers of some of Winstanley's old acquaintances, it is striking to see how much had changed since the days of the digging. John Fielder, the Kingston separatist whom Winstanley had supported in 1649, refused to yield in the face of Restoration persecution: throughout the 1660s he was the leading figure among Kingston's Quakers, he held regular meetings at his house and was frequently arrested.[49] Several of the Surrey ministers who had opposed the Diggers were ejected for nonconformity after the Restoration. Among them was Parson Platt, Winstanley's old foe in Cobham, who was presented at quarter sessions for refusing to read the Book of Common Prayer, and ejected from his West Horsley living in 1662. While Winstanley was serving as a churchwarden in Cobham, Platt was leading a risky life, sheltering nonconformists and preaching to the many Presbyterians and Independents who gathered at conventicles held at his new home in Godalming.[50] Winstanley was not the only former Digger whose career took an unusual turn at the Restoration. Henry Bickerstaffe, who had been imprisoned in Kingston in 1649, became keeper of the town's gaol in September 1661. But his replacement by another gaoler the following year suggests that he may have found it more difficult than Winstanley to conform to the restored church.[51] Perhaps closer to the spirit of the original Diggers was Thomas Starr, a former Digger who was presented in 1665 for refusing to assist Cobham's constable in breaking up a Quaker meeting in the parish.[52] We may see something of the old spirit too in the case of the 'very poor labouring Man' who in 1670 was arrested at a Quaker meeting in Walton. Since he was too poor to pay a fine, he had his spade distrained 'for lack of other Goods'. Having decided that he could not work to maintain his family without his spade, he handed his youngest child over to the parish officers for them to care of, 'Upon which they returned him the Child again, and his Spade to work for it'.[53]

Winstanley's later life was dogged by uncertainty and by complex legal disputes. In June 1660 his past caught up with him when Edward Lewis, an executor of the will of Richard Aldworth, with whom Winstanley had traded in the years 1641–3, came to his house at Cobham and threatened legal action unless he paid substantial debts that were said to be outstanding at the time of Aldworth's death. Winstanley tried to buy time, apparently promising to pay any sums that Aldworth's former servants could show were still owed. Proceedings were dropped, but after further delays they were resumed and Winstanley was arrested. He countered by launching an action against Lewis and others in the Court of Chancery, disputing their sums and claiming that all his debts to Aldworth had been paid long before. His opponents were, he claimed, attempting to take advantage of the fact that most of his account books had been 'torne lost and defaced' during 'the tyme of the late wars' – perhaps a reference to events in 1649 rather than to the Civil War itself. He also argued that the he should be protected by the statute of limitations.[54]

It seems that the court found in Winstanley's favour, and that by early 1662 proceedings against him had been abandoned. The successful outcome may have owed something to Winstanley's ability to draw on family connections, for the lawyer who took on his case was his kinsman James Winstanley of Gray's Inn.[55] James Winstanley was by far the most successful of the Winstanleys who came from Wigan to London in the decades before the Civil War. He had built up a substantial estate, partly through money lending and astute purchases of land from impoverished royalist families, and from 1653 to 1662 was recorder of Leicester. He was father-in-law of Silius Titus, the anti-Cromwellian plotter who in 1657 had helped the Leveller Edward Sexby produce *Killing Noe Murder*, the extraordinary tyrannicide tract dedicated to its principal target, Oliver Cromwell.[56] The legal action against Lewis was not the only occasion when Winstanley turned to his kinsman for help, for James helped to save his Cobham home when, in the later 1650s, his parents-in-law unexpectedly found themselves in danger of losing all their estate and possessions.

There were signs as early as 1652 that all was not well with the King family. In August of that year Giles Hickes, who was married to Susan Winstanley's sister Mary, died owing his father-in-law £200. Hickes, a minister's son, was a former naval surgeon who had served on the flagship of the Earl of Warwick, the parliamentarian naval commander. After William King was appointed surgeon at St Bartholomew's Hospital in 1643, his reversion of a surgeon's place at St Thomas's Hospital passed to Hickes, and the latter became surgeon there in 1649. It was only a matter of days after Hickes's death that King launched a suit in London's Mayor's Court to recover the £200 from his newly widowed daughter. It is possible that this was a fictitious suit, designed to protect Mary from Hickes's other creditors; we know, for instance, that several of the St Thomas's governors had lent Hickes money and therefore refused to pay his last quarter's salary when he died. But it is also possible, as Robert Dalton assumed when he first discussed the case, that this was in fact a genuine family feud and that King was determined to wrest the money from his daughter. Whatever the truth of the matter, we know that Winstanley soon became involved in the case, for in November he and William Forder, a son-in-law of the Digger John Coulton, appraised Hickes's goods by order of the court. The court awarded King execution of the goods and chattels, with Winstanley and Forder serving as pledges for the restitution.[57]

William King's eyesight had by now begun to fail, and by May 1654 his work as a surgeon at St Bartholomew's was being undertaken by his assistant Robert Arris. In February 1656 he resigned his surgeon's place and was granted a pension because of his blindness. Susan King had been busy with her own career as a midwife, and was absent from home for lengthy periods. Her husband, 'being often alone and desolate at his house' and 'very aged and infirme', took into his house in St Bartholomew-the-Less a young musician, John Stone, who was to live with him for six years. Stone seems to have been looked upon as a worthy suitor for the Kings' unmarried daughter Sarah, and he later claimed to have taught her or her sister 'to play soe well upon the harpsicon as that her teaching was well worth the sum of one hundred pounds'. In 1655 William and Susan King were faced with a lawsuit brought by Robert Gill, a London surgeon who had married their daughter Christian, and who was intent on forcing them to pay the very generous marriage portion they had promised. Their other daughters and sons-in-law had objected to the size of the portion, and were also said to be threatening legal action. William King, who was now nearly 80 and blind, deaf and 'weake in body and mynd', was persuaded to take swift action to protect his and Susan's property and ensure that their children could not 'get their estate from them in their lifetime'. In April or May 1655 their Cobham copyhold lands were surrendered to the use of Stone and his heirs, and Stone also gained possession of the leases to their London house. In March 1656 King sold Stone all his household goods and retired to Cobham, where Susan and Gerrard Winstanley were living. King

clearly assumed that he was making his house and lands over to
Stone in trust, but the relevant articles were badly drafted and
suggested an absolute transfer of ownership. Stone surrendered
the London leases to St Bartholomew's Hospital, and in May
1656 a new lease was made out in his name. He made room in
the house for Sarah and for Susan King, when the latter returned
from working in the west country, but after William King came
to stay Stone's new tenant had him arrested. King's attempts to
persuade Stone to return the deeds and writings were, by his
own account, met with threats to leave him without a groat,
to have him cast into prison – 'and there he shall rott' – and to
have Susan made homeless.[58]

The dispute was deeply worrying for the elderly Kings, whose
estate had been 'laboured for and gotten over their lifetimes by
their hard labour and profession'. At one point they accused
their daughter Sarah of siding with Stone, and William King
lamented the loss of a 'faire Library' that included historical,
religious and medical works to the value of £80 and his own
prized manuscript notes on surgery. It seems that it was Gerrard
and Susan Winstanley who stepped in to help rescue the Kings'
property and their own inheritance. They managed to get the
surrender of the Cobham copyhold, of which they were the
tenants, back into the hands of the Kings, and a surrender made
in 1657 ensured that the estate would go to them after the Kings'
deaths, provided that they paid £50 to a nominee of William or
Susan King. At the beginning of 1658 William and Susan King
launched a legal action against Stone, their case being handled
by the lawyer James Winstanley. The action was successful, the
court eventually deciding that the Kings' property had passed
to Stone in trust, and that it was not his to dispose of at will.
Susan King had, however, died before the case was resolved,
and, although Sarah effected a temporary reconciliation between
Stone and her father, Stone still refused to hand back the lease of
the Kings' London house. In 1663 he was said to be threatening
to go abroad, taking the lease with him, if attempts were made
to make him pay his debts to King.[59]

The successful outcome of the case was clearly to Winstanley's
advantage. The Cobham property was now secure, and the

Kings' gratitude was evident in the terms of the 1657 surrender. They had apparently originally wanted the estate settled in trust for all their daughters, but in 1657 it was Susan and Gerrard who benefited. Gerrard would also be allowed to keep hold of the estate if Susan died before him, and if he and Susan had no children it could, unusually, pass to children of his from a later marriage. When William King drew up his will in 1664, he confirmed the terms of the surrender and nominated Sarah King to be the recipient of the £50 to be paid by Winstanley if he wished to keep the estate. None of King's other children received anything so substantial.[60]

We know from William King's will that Susan Winstanley had died by 1664, though no record of her burial or date of death has been found. King himself died in 1666 in Hornchurch in Essex, where his daughter Sarah was living. The Cobham copyhold will then have passed to Winstanley and his heirs. In July 1664 Winstanley was married for a second time, in the London parish of St Giles Cripplegate. His new wife was Elizabeth Stanley or Standley, who was many years younger than him. Elizabeth was to give birth to three children: Jerrard, Elizabeth and Clement, who were baptised in Cobham parish church in 1665, 1668 and 1670 respectively. Clement was almost certainly named after the eldest son and heir of the lawyer James Winstanley, who had done so much to help Gerrard in his legal battles.[61] Gerrard's marriage to Elizabeth Stanley was however to entangle him in another series of legal actions, which were in many ways more baffling and intractable than any he had experienced before. These actions were to see Winstanley taking hold of the revenues of a major landed estate in Herefordshire, doling out an allowance to a leading civil war royalist and being forced to do business with some of the most disreputable characters that even Restoration England could produce.

Elizabeth Winstanley was the niece of Hugh Turner of Wapping Wall, who was an executor of the will of Sampson Wise of Clerkenwell. Wise's father-in-law was Fitzwilliam Coningsby of Hampton Court in Herefordshire, a former Herefordshire knight of the shire who had been expelled from the Long Parliament in 1641 as a monopolist. Coningsby had taken up arms for the

king on the outbreak of civil war, and was one of the dominant
figures in Herefordshire's royalist party. His wartime losses were
catastrophic, and after the war he had turned to Wise for help
in rebuilding his shattered estate and paying off his debts, which
amounted to several thousand pounds. When Wise died in 1663,
his executors were instructed to recover some of the money he
had ploughed into the Coningsby estates, which he estimated
at £5,700, and to pay substantial bequests out of this. Turner
did not live long enough to recover the money due to him and
his relatives, and when he drew up his will in April 1665 he
named as executor his nephew and godson Hugh Flood, and
as overseers Nicholas Kirwood, a Herefordshire attorney, and
Winstanley. Flood was under age at the time, so Winstanley was
to act as a *de facto* executor responsible for recovering the debts
owing from the vast Coningsby estates, including an annual rent
charge of £200.[62]

Turner's will is of interest for what it says about Winstanley.
Winstanley's fellow overseer, Nicholas Kirwood, was described
as 'able and honest', and was regarded by Turner as 'one
who knowes how to gett in my estate better then any other
in England'. But with Winstanley Turner felt compelled to
threaten to withhold the legacies due to him and Elizabeth if
he failed to do his best to bring in the money that was owed.[63]
Turner's comments have often seemed puzzling, but one reason
for Winstanley's apparent reluctance to act may have been the
identity of some of those with whom he would have to work.
Kirwood seems to have had a bad enough reputation, despite
what Turner said about him, and he was later described as 'a
most infamous attorney of those times'. Much worse however
was William Hill, a Herefordshire minister and trustee of
Coningsby property, who was the person with whom Winstanley
would work most closely. In the 1780s the historian Catharine
Macaulay was to describe Hill as a 'profligate abandoned
wretch'; Fitzwilliam Coningsby's grandson Thomas Lord
Coningsby went even further, calling him 'this presumptuous
monster', 'this monstrous Priest', 'this infernal Parson Hill', 'the
most wicked son that ever was born to a wicked father' and 'the
most flagrantly wicked of all priests that ever were before him,

of any sort or sect'.[64] Lord Coningsby, who himself enjoyed a reputation, as his recent biographer has noted, as 'a madman, a monster and a brutal tyrant', had strong personal motives for disliking Hill, but there were additional reasons for his distaste, for Hill was already widely seen as someone who had caused the deaths of several people for personal gain.[65]

Hill was the son of Miles Hill, a Herefordshire Baptist and parliamentarian sequestration official. During the 1650s he had become a minister and obtained a living at Standish in Gloucestershire, but he lost this after the Restoration. On 16 October 1662 he was in London when he encountered an acquaintance, Captain John Baker, who spoke incautiously to him of the impending 'slaughter and confusion of those Rogues at Whitehall'. Hill probed further, and was soon invited to meetings where he learnt of well-developed plans to raise a force of Baptists, Fifth-Monarchists and 'fighting Quakers' to murder the king and leading ministers and to return England to a commonwealth. Hill bided his time, learning more, making helpful suggestions and ingratiating himself with the conspirators: 'our conference was all of God's glory, in zeal we were up to the eyes; and I began exactly to speak the language'. Soon he had betrayed the plot to Major-General Sir Richard Browne and was instructed to play along with the conspirators and to gather further incriminating information. He continued to attend meetings, to all appearances as an enthusiastic participant, and reported back nightly to Browne. He was present when arrests were made and was one of the chief witnesses at a trial that saw six men condemned to death and four executed for high treason. None of them was a leading figure in the conspiracy and most, it seems, were guilty of little more than failing to report what they knew to the authorities. Further executions took place later. Hill wrote an account of the conspiracy and trial, and made much of his role in the affair. He was evidently proud of what he had done, and happy to be seen as the person who had helped avert the 'stupendious tragedie' intended by 'the Satanical Saints of these reforming times', and prevent 'a total destruction of King, Lords, Bishops and Gentry'. He was rewarded with a substantial cash sum and the living of Pencombe in Herefordshire, which he would hold on to until his death.[66]

During Hugh Flood's minority Winstanley dutifully administered Hugh Turner's estate and received rents and profits from Fitzwilliam Coningsby's Herefordshire lands. By an indenture of April or July 1666, made between Winstanley, Coningsby and Hill, it was agreed that the £1,850 which was said to be owed to Turner's estate should be raised, along with the rent charge of £200 a year which Turner had previously agreed with Coningsby. Winstanley also agreed to sell and assign over to Hill all the relevant deeds and estate papers to help ensure that all the money could be swiftly brought in. By his own account Winstanley received £429 5s 8d from Coningsby's tenants, repaying a quarter of this sum as an allowance to Coningsby, who throughout this time was technically a prisoner in the Fleet though allowed home in the custody of two keepers. But Winstanley and others interested in the Coningsby estates were harried by lawsuits, and in 1669, after Coningsby's death, Winstanley was a defendant in cases brought by Coningsby's executor and by the widow of Sampson Wise. In both these suits Hill was a co-defendant with Winstanley and worked closely with him.[67]

In 1667 another figure entered the scene. This was Ferdinando Gorges, a wealthy Barbados merchant and a notorious slave trader who was known as 'King of the Blacks'. Gorges had become interested in the valuable Coningsby estates and intended to marry his daughter to Fitzwilliam Coningsby's young grandson. Through Kirwood he was introduced to Hugh Flood, then an apprentice to a Clerkenwell pastry cook; Gorges took Flood to 'sundry Tavernes and Drinking places' and offered to buy out his interest for £300. He advanced him small sums of money and threatened him with arrest when they were not repaid. He also made a point of courting Winstanley, proffering great friendship, writing frequently to him and inviting him several times to his house. He praised Winstanley's 'plaine honesty' and told him that 'we doe not studye Machiavell as much as some doe'. In 1669 Gorges had William Hill imprisoned in order to recover the deeds and papers that Winstanley had signed over to him. Winstanley began to suspect that Hill's arrest was a feigned one, and that Gorges was now conspiring with Hill and Kirwood to deprive him and his relatives of their rightful share of the Coningsby revenues. No further money seems to have been forthcoming, and Winstanley claimed that the original £1,850 was still owed in 1675, along with the £200 rent charge. In that year Winstanley, along with his wife and other relatives, launched an action in Chancery against Gorges and others to recover the money. Winstanley's bill and Gorges's answer are extraordinary documents, displaying a passion that the measured language of lawyers and their clerks could not expunge. Winstanley believed that he had been duped and accused Gorges of overcoming him with 'pretences and importunities'; Gorges responded by blaming Hill – a man of 'very ill fame and reputation' – and Kirwood for making it so difficult to get money out of the Coningsby estates, and he insisted that Winstanley should be grateful for his intervention in the Coningsby affairs. He himself was, he claimed, concerned only in preserving what was left of the estate.[68]

The case was probably left unresolved, for on 10 September 1676 Winstanley, suffering from 'gripes & vomiting', died. We know something of his final few months besides what can be pieced together from the legal records relating to the Coningsby revenues. By 1675 he and Elizabeth had left Cobham and were living in the parish of St Giles-in-the-Fields in Middlesex. They occupied a substantial house with ten hearths on the 'Street Side' close to Bloomsbury Square, and Gerrard was apparently now in business as a corn chandler. Most striking is the fact that his death was recorded in the burial register of the Westminster Quakers' monthly meeting and he was buried in the newly opened Long Acre Quaker burial ground.[69] It is sometimes thought that it was Elizabeth – who is known to have become a Quaker – who ensured that he received a Quaker burial. But the records of the Westminster monthly meeting at the Savoy show that Winstanley himself attended meetings. In July 1676, for instance, he was one of the 30 present at the marriage of James Carter and Elizabeth Aplin, and the first whose name was listed.[70] It seems clear that by 1676, if not earlier, Winstanley had finally embraced Quakerism. In doing so, he was following the example of Levellers such as John Lilburne and also several of his fellow Diggers. Elizabeth later married a Quaker, Giles Stuchbury, and her will, which was drawn up in 1708, shows that she died a Quaker. Her sons Jerrard and Clement – and possibly her daughter Elizabeth – had predeceased her, so she directed that much of her property should be put in trust for the relief of the Quaker poor.[71]

Gerrard Winstanley's life, from his arrival in London as a young man to those last battles over the revenues of the Coningsby estates had been an extraordinary one, and unusually well documented for someone who was not obviously from a landed family. His prose writings, which place him among the finest writers of the age, his activities as a Digger and the striking religious and political ideas he expressed in the years 1648–52 have ensured that interest in him remains strong; future archival discoveries and reinterpretations of his writings will no doubt add more to the picture we now have of him. But it is always important to remember that he was not always a well-known figure, and that until relatively recently few people knew anything of his life and ideas. The story of Winstanley's posthumous reputation is an important one, and needs to be considered in its own right. It can also help us to understand how Winstanley has in recent decades come to be seen as one of England's greatest radicals.

5

Winstanley's Legacy

Twenty years after the collapse of the Soviet Union, the memorial obelisk to great thinkers and revolutionaries was still standing in Moscow's Alexander Gardens, though there was talk of restoring it to its original purpose as a monument to the Romanovs. On 31 October 2008 an unusual act of pilgrimage took place, when Richard Reynolds, founder of www.GuerillaGardening.org, planted Oxford red tulip bulbs close to the obelisk in honour of Gerrard Winstanley, the 'seventeenth-century guerrilla gardener'.[1] Twenty-first-century guerrilla gardeners are not alone in claiming Winstanley as one of their precursors. It should not be surprising to find that the origins of freeganism and squatting are often said to date back to the activities of Winstanley and the Diggers, and that modern champions of urban allotments have come to see Winstanley as 'a key activist, probably the earliest' in the international allotment movement.[2]

It is, understandably, as a pioneer of radical land and environmental activism that Winstanley is most often remembered today. In May 1996, the MP Tony Benn hailed the decision of Newbury bypass campaigners to plant fruit and vegetables along the line of the proposed road as proof that they had 'rooted their campaign deep into our own history of radical dissent and linked themselves with the Diggers of 1649'.[3] Other commentators on anti-roads and airport protests made similar connections. The campaign that drew most heavily in the 1990s on memories of Winstanley and the Diggers was The Land is Ours (TLIO). In 1995 the emergent TLIO very consciously emulated the actions of the Diggers when activists set up a camp at the disused Wisley airfield in Surrey and briefly invaded the fairways of St George's Hill golf course. The campaigner and author George Monbiot, then a leading figure in TLIO, spoke

Digger related posters, fliers and postcards 1985–2012. Winstanley's writings continue to inspire activists. Credit: John Gurney.

forcefully of the land access issues which seemed as pressing then as in 1649. Monbiot's identification with Winstanley was so strong that a writer in the *New Statesman* could suggest that he was 'rapidly being dubbed the new Gerrard Winstanley'.[4] Four years later, on the 350th anniversary of the start of the Digger experiment, activists associated with TLIO gathered in Walton before marching to St George's Hill, where they set up their tents, yurt and compost toilets on North Surrey Water Company land near the summit. They brought with them Andrew Whittle's newly carved Digger memorial stone, and among their demands was that a permanent site be found for the stone and that there should be guaranteed rights of access to the site and elsewhere on the hill. The activists planned a 'Diggers' Open Day', complete with 'Diggers' soup and other vegetarian feed', and were visited by attendees at a Digger conference being held in Walton and Weybridge, including the veteran Labour politician Michael Foot. The occupation lasted from the 3rd until the afternoon of 15 April, when the site was abandoned before a possession order could be put into effect. Other land occupations followed, among them a 'Diggers' Land Grab' of an old hospital site in Norfolk. This quickly became known as 'Kett's Camp', in commemoration of the 450th anniversary of Kett's Norfolk Rebellion that fell fortuitously in the same year.[5]

It is often thought that attempts by activists to claim inspiration from Winstanley and the Diggers is a recent phenomenon, but pilgrimages to St George's Hill have been taking place for more than a hundred years. It was on 10 February 1908 that Alexander Stewart Gray, leader of Manchester's hunger marchers, announced his intention of travelling to Cobham, 'where in the Commonwealth days Jerrard Winstanley "grabbed" a piece of land and taught the people how to grow their own food'. This was, he believed, 'the highest thought reached in Cromwell's time, and I want to kindle my torch on the very site of Winstanley's exploit. We shall throw up a mound and deposit an ivy wreath.'[6] Stewart Gray is almost completely forgotten today, but he was a familiar figure on the political stage in Edwardian England. An Edinburgh barrister and Writer of the Signet, he abandoned his legal career to become a mystic and hermit before throwing in his

lot with the unemployed and pioneering land grabbing, hunger
marches and hunger strikes. In July 1906 Gray and others seized
church land at Levenshulme in Manchester, where they set up
camp and hoped to 'teach the unemployed to dig'. Soon other
camps had appeared in Manchester, Bradford and London.[7] The
leaders of the land grabs were said to be boasting of 'having
gone back to the days of Cromwell' – no doubt a reference to
the Diggers.[8] Gray defended his actions at Levenshulme with
Winstanley-like language, claiming that his mission was 'to
preach the Scriptural gospel of "Back to the land" to all people,
both by physical example and oral effort, and by discussion of
eternal laws with the many truth-seekers who visit us'. Churches
were, he insisted, 'organisations of the rich who deny manhood
its natural rights' and 'stink in the nostrils of the poor'; they fail
to recognise that the cure for social ills is 'the granting to the
people of liberty, which I ... hold to be impossible of realisation
apart from the right of man to support himself at first hand on
the land'.[9] He later suggested that the coming millennium would
be a time when 'every man would return to the soil, with a desire
not to live upon his brother, but to live upon his father, nature
– to live more simple, humble, and beautiful lives'.[10]

In February 1907 Gray was instrumental in the establishment
of a land colony on a 40-acre site on Chat Moss, which had
the reluctant backing of Manchester's distress committee.
When support for further colonies was refused, Gray turned to
petitioning king and parliament on behalf of the unemployed,
invading the pulpit of Manchester Cathedral and leading a
hunger march to London, which took place in January 1908.[11]
It was after he had announced his plan to settle part of Windsor
Great Park as a colony for the unemployed, and had addressed
the boys of Eton College on the unemployment problem, that
Gray made his pilgrimage to Cobham. Although St George's
Hill was then still open land, and not yet developed for housing,
Gray and his companions were unfortunate in turning up on
11 February, the day of the hill's annual closure. Unable to
gain access to set up his memorial to Winstanley, Gray took a
growing cabbage from a cottage garden and planted it in protest

outside the main entrance to the hill. A few days later he began a hunger strike.[12]

The visit to St George's Hill may not have been successful, but it prompted newspapers to discuss the activities of 'Winstanley the Leveller' who had 'led a party of Cromwellian unemployed to dig'. The *Manchester Guardian* in particular thought that 'the views of the diggers are especially interesting'.[13] Gray continued his activities on behalf of the unemployed throughout 1908, and set up a 'Freedom Camp' in Cardiff; in the autumn he was arrested at demonstrations at Tower Hill and Trafalgar Square, and he famously interrupted afternoon service in Canterbury Cathedral.[14] After failing to secure nomination for election to parliament as an unemployed candidate, Gray turned to art and squatting.[15] He later went on to establish an artists' commune in Primrose Hill, frequented by, among others, David Bomberg, William Roberts and Jacob Epstein, and he eventually retired to a cottage in Essex where he received regular financial support from his friend Augustus John. He died in 1937. Epstein thought he 'resembled a Tolstoy gone wrong'; Roberts fittingly remembered him as 'the first of the "Hippies" or "Squatters"'.[16]

Stewart Gray's example serves as a reminder of the ways in which fluctuating levels of interest in Winstanley have so often reflected the perceived contemporary relevance of his ideas. In the fallow period between 1660 and the 1890s his memory was, as we have seen, kept alive partly by hostile clergymen keen to prove that he was the true originator of Quakerism, and also by the few Quakers and dissenters who were fortunate enough to stumble across his works. Winstanley's writings were also known to some Universalists – those who believed that all would or might be saved.[17] Much more, however, was known about the Diggers than about Winstanley himself. Bulstrode Whitelocke's manuscript 'Annals', later published as the *Memorials of the English Affairs*, had included a lengthy extract from *The Declaration and Standard of the Levellers of England* (1649), the work that described Winstanley and Everard's meeting with Fairfax in April 1649.[18] This extract gave the impression that it was Everard who was the leading figure among the Diggers, and most subsequent writers assumed the same. A succession of writers – among them David Hume, William Godwin, François Guizot, John Forster and Thomas Carlyle – made use of Whitelocke to describe the activities of the Diggers, but none of them showed much interest in Winstanley.[19]

It was, of course, in the 1890s that attention turned once again to Winstanley. Eduard Bernstein, whose account of Winstanley was published in 1895, was the first to write about him in detail, but he was by no means the only scholar to be working on him at this time. The interest taken in Winstanley by late-nineteenth-century British radicals reflected the immense importance of the land question in late-Victorian Britain. Henry George's proposals for the taxation of land values, or a single tax, had made great headway in Britain, as had more radical arguments in favour of the state ownership of land. Still more radical were the direct-action 'back-to-the-land' enthusiasts who set about establishing self-sustaining settlements in rural areas, among them the anarchist Clousden Hill Free Communist and Cooperative Colony outside Newcastle (established 1895), and the Tolstoyan colonies at Purleigh in Essex (1896) and Whiteway in Gloucestershire (1898).[20] Lewis Berens, who first published on Winstanley in 1898, is often described as a Quaker, but he was in fact a noted single-taxer, active in land nationalisation campaigns in Britain and South Australia, and the author of influential works on political and land reform. Also heavily involved in land reform was J. Morrison Davidson, the barrister, journalist and inveterate political campaigner whose writings on Winstanley were to be particularly influential among the British left. The trade unionist Tom Mann learned about Winstanley through Davidson, and it is likely that Stewart Gray did too.[21] Others who picked up on the significance of Winstanley's writings for modern land campaigns included Joseph Clayton, who in 1910 was able to assert that the Digger's 'social teaching on the land question has thousands of disciples in Great Britain today'.[22]

It is in the mid twentieth century that we see the emergence of the firm and lasting association between Winstanley and the modern British left. Particularly important was the interest in him taken by figures on the left of the Labour Party, among them Fenner Brockway, Eric Heffer, Michael Foot and Tony Benn.

Brockway discovered the Levellers as a teenager, but his lively and affectionate portrait of *Britain's First Socialists* was not published until he was in his ninety-second year.[23] Tony Benn's interest in Winstanley and the Diggers developed rapidly in the 1970s. He was given a private tutorial on Levellers and Diggers in the House of Commons tea room by the MP Jack Mendelson, a former university lecturer, and was soon speaking about them at the annual Burford Leveller Day celebrations.[24] Another MP who knew a good deal about Diggers and Levellers was Walter Padley (1916–84), who was brought up near Burford. He was described in *The Times* in 1961 as having 'a prodigious memory', which he drew on to recall footballers' names and 'to quote long, fine passages from the little-known writings of the Leveller, Gerrard Winstanley'.[25]

For the Labour left, the story of the Diggers was often treated as part of a broader, alternative popular history, one intended to show up the inadequacy of history as taught in schools, and aimed at recovering Britain's own, largely hidden socialist heritage. To Benn, the Diggers had 'established the clear outlines of democratic socialism', while for Heffer, remembering the Digger and Leveller movements was important in reminding us that 'socialism in Britain is not a foreign import, not an alien influence, grafted on to the British people from outside. It is inherently British, in reality as British as the Union Jack or the hymn "Abide With Me"'.[26] With the exception of Brockway's work, there was rarely any great distinction made in these accounts between Levellers and Diggers, and the two groups were often presented as related elements in the long tradition of radical, popular protest stretching from the Peasants' Revolt, through the English Revolution radicals and Chartists, to the present.

The distinction between Diggers and Levellers was, however, of much greater importance to scholars associated with the Communist Party in the 1940s and 1950s. These scholars included the historians Christopher Hill and Margaret James and the academic and future cabinet minister Edmund Dell. The scientist Joseph Needham, though probably never a Party member, might also be identified with this group.[27] Communist

Party interest in the Diggers is usually seen as deriving from the Popular Front politics of the 1930s, but this is slightly misleading. The classic Popular Front historical text, A.L. Morton's 1938 *A People's History of England*, was in its first edition quite dismissive of the Diggers. For Morton it was 'the backward turning face of the Leveller movement that we see in the Diggers, and their pacifism was a cause of hesitation and inactivity in moments of crisis'.[28] It was only in the following decade, and especially around the time of the English Revolution tercentenary celebrations in 1949, that the Communist Party's attitude towards Winstanley and his companions became wholly favourable. The Party's commemoration of the tercentenary of 1649 was marked by the publication of a series of essays in *The Modern Quarterly*, including Edmund Dell's on Winstanley and the Diggers, which provided a detailed analysis of Winstanley's programme and intellectual development and sought to trace his transition from anarchist to supporter of state action to achieve his ends.[29] Also to appear in 1949 was Hill and Dell's selection of texts from the revolutionary years, *The Good Old Cause*, which contained a chapter on the Diggers celebrating their commitment to a communist future.[30] Morton's views on the Diggers were revised, and he now praised them for their 'remarkably foresighted anticipation of the essentials of our own socialist conceptions'.[31]

It is perhaps not surprising that members of the Stalin-era Communist Party Historians' Group, with their concern to recover England's radical past, should seek to make use of renewed interest in the Diggers in order to reclaim this most radical and proletarian of social movements.[32] The Diggers readily lent themselves to the Party's historical propaganda work, a process, as Hill put it in 1950, of 'Marxists ... restoring their past to the people', or of recovering 'part of their heritage of which they have been robbed'.[33] With their distinction of having 'put forward a communist programme', Winstanley and his fellow Diggers had a secure place in the history of the people's centuries-long struggles against oppression. There was no reason to doubt the legitimacy of Winstanley's inclusion on Lenin's monument to great thinkers and revolutionaries. But

Winstanley's promotion by the Communist Party came at the expense of the Levellers, who soon faded from view. The Levellers were now seen as advocates of 'petty bourgeois' democracy, and their aims, however laudable, were ones that could never have been fully realised. By the 1650s, it was suggested, most of their leaders had 'either made money and were absorbed into the bourgeoisie, or relapsed into a mystical quietism'. Their wasted struggle for civil liberties and the limiting of state power could be contrasted with Winstanley and the Diggers' much more realistic recognition that freedom could mean nothing without the prior establishment of economic and social equality.[34]

The Levellers were not helped by the fact that much recent work on them had been undertaken in America, particularly by scholars keen to stress their contribution to the development of religious toleration and liberal constitutional theory.[35] But not all Marxists were happy with the displacement of the Levellers by Winstanley. The case for the Levellers was first put from a Trotskyist perspective by C.L.R. James, writing under the pseudonym G.F. Eckstein in the *Fourth International* in 1949. For James, the Levellers were a genuinely autonomous revolutionary movement and had been demoted by the Communists because there was no room for them in their 'bureaucratic, authoritarian conception of society and politics'. In place of the Levellers the 'Stalinists' had, he claimed, chosen to champion two heroes of bourgeois revolution – John Milton and Oliver Cromwell – and had rescued from oblivion an interesting but obscure figure in Gerrard Winstanley. The Diggers were, compared with the Levellers, few in number and weak; Winstanley was 'a man of undoubted genius',

> But to take Winstanley as characteristic of the revolution and to ignore the Levellers on his behalf is such a violation of historical facts, historical method and the living class struggle as can come only from an organic hostility to any independent revolutionary movement of the masses.[36]

James was by no means an isolated voice, for echoes of his doubts could be found in the work of later socialist historians, most notably Brian Manning and Norah Carlin. Manning was

Hill's pupil, and is often lumped together with him, but their Marxism had very different roots.[37] Manning was, like Carlin, always more sympathetic than Hill to the Levellers, and more ambivalent about the Diggers. While Hill was one of those who welcomed C.B. Macpherson's Marxist reinterpretation of the Levellers as possessive individualists, Manning took Macpherson to task for misinterpreting Marx.[38] He also drew attention to the disparity between Digger aims and the interests of small peasants whose livelihood depended on regulated access to the commons, and he highlighted what he saw as 'the gulf between the Diggers and any real potential of the peasantry for revolutionary action'.[39]

Alongside these contrasting Marxist approaches to Winstanley, anarchist and left-libertarian readings continued to develop from the mid twentieth century onwards. In the 1960s these were boosted by the publication of George Woodcock's influential *Anarchism*. This first appeared in 1962, and achieved widespread sales after it was reissued the following year as a Penguin paperback. In this work Woodcock built on his 1944 account of Winstanley and the Diggers, and developed his argument that Winstanley should be seen as a forerunner of anarchism rather than as a proto Marxist. In response to the attempts by Marxists to claim Winstanley 'as their ancestor', Woodcock insisted that

there is nothing Marxian about the peasant paradise that Winstanley envisages in *The New Law of Righteousness*. Its communism is entirely libertarian, and the effort of Winstanley and his friends on St George's Hill stands at the beginning of the anarchist tradition of direct action.[40]

It seems clear that Woodcock's work, with its presentation of Winstanley and his fellow Diggers as early anarchists, made a significant contribution – alongside Hill's work – to the popular revival of interest in Winstanley which took place in the 1960s and '70s.

The Diggers certainly caught the mood of the 1960s radical counter-culture. It was in 1966 that a new group of Diggers appeared in San Francisco's Haight-Ashbury district. Emerging from the San Francisco Mime Group and Artists' Liberation

Front, the Haight-Ashbury Diggers became well known for handing out food to the poor, establishing free stores, clinics and legal services, and engaging in anti-capitalist street theatre and propaganda events. The choice of name was not accidental: the Digger Peter Berg later recalled that it was Billy Murcott, who had been 'reading about social revolutionary groups in history', who first suggested that they call themselves Diggers. The example of Winstanley's Diggers seemed appropriate to these 'communal shock troops of the early hip era', as did their name: 'We also took the word *digger* to mean to *dig*, as in "I dig it"'.[41] The Haight-Ashbury Diggers, who were described at the time as 'an amorphous, shifting, and sometimes contentious amalgam of ex-political radicals, psychedelic mystics, Ghandians, and Brechtian avant-garde thespians', were soon inspiring Digger groups elsewhere in the United States and Canada, and their ideas and actions influenced the emergent commune movement and the New York Yippies.[42]

The British underground press had picked up on the 'mystery-shrouded Haight-Ashbury group' by February 1967, and knew that their name came from 'a 17th-century group of communal farmers in England'.[43] Digger groups also soon appeared, or re-appeared, in Britain, among them the Hapt Diggers in 1967 and the Coventry Diggers, based on a self-service food store, in 1968.[44] Best known were the Digger groups associated with the charismatic Sid Rawle, including the Hyde Park Diggers and the Digger Action Movement, with its 'Tribe of the Sun' inner core. Rawle later told the filmmaker Kevin Brownlow that he knew nothing of the links to Winstanley when the Hyde Park Diggers were formed in 1967: he was, he claimed, simply copying the San Francisco Diggers, and 'it took us a few months to discover the San Francisco Diggers were taking off the British Diggers'.[45] The reluctance to identify too closely with the original Diggers may also have reflected the Hyde Park Diggers' initial strategy. Rawle felt that an urban community should first be established, out of which farm communities (which he acknowledged to be an 'essential part of the Digger programme') would only later develop. A rapid retreat to the countryside might isolate the group, and he feared that too few of the Diggers had sufficient rural knowledge or skills to succeed in getting working communities in the countryside up and running. Rural communities needed careful planning, and there were hopes that urban Digger settlements could be used to prepare people for a move to the country. Rawle was also keen to emphasise the need to establish workshops to produce goods for the open market in 'a syndicalist atmosphere', and he warned that 'we cannot go back 100 years or 1,000 and this type of nihilist thinking can only do harm to the Diggers'.[46]

The Hyde Park Diggers took part in the revived Aldermaston march of April 1968 and in the following month's May Day march from Tower Hill to Westminster. In 1969 they participated in the famous London Street Commune squat at 144 Piccadilly. Rawle was also present when Al Krebs and other academics addressed a 'Diggers' Symposium' at London's Anti-University; the meeting broke up in disorder, with activists claiming that they 'are not interested in theory and they do not need theory'.[47] In 1970 Rawle was offered the use of the uninhabited Dorinish Island in Clew Bay, County Mayo by John Lennon, who had bought it in 1967. Here Rawle and members of the Digger Action Movement established a self-supporting settlement, digging wells, building a store and planting crops.[48] The settlement lasted three years, though Rawle and other Dorinish Diggers took time off in 1971 to set up a food kitchen at the first Glastonbury festival, apparently paid for by the model Jean Shrimpton.[49] Rawle went on to be active in the squatting and free festival movements, in the 1980s Peace Convoy and Molesworth Rainbow Village, and in the Rainbow 2000 camps. It seems fitting that he was given the part of the Ranter Laurence Clarkson in Kevin Brownlow and Andrew Mollo's film *Winstanley*.[50]

The Digger name was put to a rather different use in 1974, when Susan Inkster stood as a Digger candidate for Cambridge in the February general election. Hers was essentially a left-environmentalist programme, and one that differed markedly and very deliberately from that of Teddy Goldsmith, who was standing as the 'People' candidate for Eye in Suffolk.[51] The Diggers called for decentralisation, limits to economic growth, self-sufficiency in food and energy, and the conservation of the world's natural resources. Local issues were also addressed, with the Diggers opposing the expansion of the University and the destruction of Cambridge homes for offices, car parks and supermarkets.[52] During the election campaign Inkster was reported in the press to be describing her politics as 'Digger' and to have 'invoked the name of Winstanley', though the 'new Diggers' were also said to 'regard the history as an analogy rather than an exact parallel'. Their election poster bore the words 'Danger: politicians at work', and their placards 'Dig for victory'.[53]

Inkster received 369 out of 59,422 votes cast at the election. This was, she thought, 'pretty good' considering that no more than £20 had been spent on publicity and that her campaign had lasted for only ten days: 'This is only the start. People in Cambridge will be hearing much more of the Diggers in the near future.'[54] When interviewed the following year, she refused to rule out 'a return of Diggery', and of Winstanley's ideas, to the Cambridge political scene.[55] Martin Richards, the Cambridge academic who served as Inkster's election agent, argued that the Diggers had 'achieved something ... at several party meetings we turned the discussion to real issues, and we got a lot of good local press coverage'.[56] By mid 1975, however, Inkster's attention was focused to the 'impressively Winstanley-esque enterprise' of the Arjuna wholefood cooperative in Mill Road, Cambridge, while other Diggers were busy establishing 'the largest agricultural commune in Britain' on an abandoned farm outside Bodmin. The commune's constitution was said to be based on Winstanley's *Law of Freedom*.[57] There were no Digger candidates standing in Cambridge in the November 1974 or 1979 general elections, and in 1983 it was the mainstream Ecology Party that cited the Diggers in its general election manifesto.[58]

Winstanley's appeal in the 1970s was, as the example of the Cambridge Diggers demonstrates, associated increasingly with the emergent green movement.[59] We can see this too in the Winstanley who featured so importantly in Christopher Hill's *The World Turned Upside Down*. Hill had left the Communist Party in 1957, and 15 years later he produced his classic work of history from below, a work in which the modern image of Winstanley assumed its now familiar shape. Winstanley's insights

into the Fall and the corruption of the earth were now shown
to have profound contemporary relevance for a generation
becoming alarmed by the destruction of the environment and
by threats of nuclear war: the late twentieth century's 'landscape
made hideous by neon signs, advertisements, pylons, wreckage
of automobiles', and its poisoned seas, polluted atmosphere and
'nuclear bombs which can "waste and destroy" to an extent
that Winstanley never dreamed of', were all drawn into the
discussion.[60] The Winstanley of *The World Turned Upside Down*,
and of Hill's 1973 Pelican edition of Winstanley's writings, spoke
powerfully to the new social movements of the 1960s and '70s,
and to those members of a younger generation who increasingly
questioned the achievements of post-war capitalism and rejected
its values.[61]

Winstanley was also becoming much better known through
novels, plays and films. The starting point was the publication
in 1961 of *Comrade Jacob*, the novel about the Diggers by
the author and academic David Caute, who had learnt about
Winstanley in tutorials with Hill at Oxford.[62] Caute's novel was
dramatised by Christopher Williams for a BBC Studio Four
production in September 1962, and in 1969 Sussex University's
new Gardner Centre for the Arts opened with a version by the
radical playwright John McGrath.[63] Caute's novel also famously
formed the basis for Brownlow and Mollo's extraordinary
1975 film *Winstanley*. The original screenplay for the film was
provided by Caute, but after many changes were made during
production – including ones which, he felt, drained Winstanley
of much of his religious fervour – he withdrew his name from
the credits.[64] The film, though never widely distributed, gained
a ferociously loyal following, and many were the groups and
societies which struggled to find the correct projectors to show it
as the directors intended. Brownlow and Mollo were scrupulous
in their attention to period detail, using correctly made clothing,
historic armour and rare breed animals, and tracking down
unrestored seventeenth-century buildings for use in the film.[65]
Winstanley was seen by relatively few people in British cinemas,
but it was well received in France and Italy. The apparent Soviet
indifference to the film was blamed by Brownlow on lack of

support from the British delegation at the Moscow Film Festival, but one wonders whether the close resemblance between his Diggers and peasant Tolstoyan communalists – mention of whom was virtually impossible in the Soviet Union before 1988 – may also have played a part. The film's Diggers were certainly unlike the advanced communists traditionally portrayed in Soviet historiography.[66]

The numbers of cinema-goers who saw *Winstanley* may have been small, but theatre audiences in the 1970s were also able to learn more about Winstanley and the Diggers. They appeared fleetingly in Caryl Churchill's *Light Shining in Buckinghamshire*, first performed in 1976, and in Keith Dewhurst's *The World Turned Upside Down*, put on by the National Theatre in 1978.[67] During the 1980s several small-scale theatre productions, including the Brighton Actors' Workshop production of Chris Stagg and Paul Hodson's Digger play *The World Turned Upside Down*, were performed in community and pub theatres across the country.[68] When Churchill's *Light Shining* was revived as a National Theatre mobile production in 1996, the accompanying programme, poster and publicity material made much of the play's references to the Diggers; the programme contained stirring quotes from Winstanley's writings, and explicit connections were made between the Diggers of 1649–50 and today's 'new Diggers', who 'all over the country defend the land against the advance of the machine'.[69] In reality, Churchill's play contained only one brief scene – or one-and-a-half pages in a 60-page script – in which the Diggers took centre stage. Churchill had sought to capture, in all its vitality and heterodoxy, the spirit of the counter-cultural moment of 1647–49, and to explore what she described as 'the complexity of the aims and conflicts' of those who stood 'to the left of Parliament'. By 1996, however, it was Winstanley and the Diggers on whom the attention largely rested, and with whom a theatre audience was presumably most expected to identify.[70]

Winstanley has been assigned many roles in the century or so after his rediscovery by the left. He has been remembered as revolutionary thinker and activist, champion of a native radical political tradition, mystic, materialist, radical democrat, proto

Marxist, precursor of Henry George, anarchist, land grabber, squatter, pioneer green, peace campaigner, social entrepreneur and proponent of non-violent popular direct action. Each of these roles has at least some basis in fact, and draws on aspects of Winstanley's writings and of the Digger story. It would be wrong to insist that any one of them is wholly unwarranted, but each, with its singular focus, can tend to distortion by providing only a partial reading of Winstanley's complex ideas. It is perfectly understandable why Winstanley's writings and example should have become such an important reference point for modern social movements, particularly given the regular use made by activists since the 1970s of static protest camps. From Torness in the 1970s, to the 1980s' peace camps, the 1990s' eco-protest camps and the twenty-first-century Occupy movement, protestors have often emulated the Diggers in occupying a fixed site and attempting to hold out peacefully against hostile interests.[71]

The remarkable history of Leon Rosselson's 'World Turned Upside Down' song tells us much about where Winstanley now sits in the modern radical imagination.[72] It has been memorably recorded by, amongst others, Rosselson, Dick Gaughan and Billy Bragg, and it has been regularly performed by Roy Bailey on his 'The Writing on the Wall' tours with Tony Benn.[73] In the 1970s and 1980s the song quickly became a familiar protest anthem, adopted (and in some cases adapted) by Greenham women, miners' support groups and anti-roads protestors. Versions of it have been sung by activists across the world – and once even broadcast on radio as a traditional anthem of Nicaraguan coffee-bean pickers.[74] Performed by Rosselson at the foot of St George's Hill and at the Diggers' rally in 1999, it has remained popular among activists in the twenty-first century. Rosselson, fittingly, performed the song in November 2011 at the Occupy London camp outside St Paul's Cathedral, and four months later he sang it to Wellingborough's Independent Socialists when they gathered at their second annual festival to celebrate their town's Digger heritage.[75]

As Winstanley has gained status in the revolutionary pantheon, other, once more famous radicals have gradually been displaced. The shifting fortunes of past radicals may be illustrated by comparing Winstanley with John Hampden. Hampden, the great civil war parliamentarian who resisted the payment of ship money, and who died from wounds sustained when fighting Prince Rupert's forces at Chalgrove Field, was for many generations celebrated as one of England's greatest radicals. Some activists named their sons after him, others joined Hampden clubs or placed portraits of him on their walls; the Chartist Thomas Cooper even drew his own pictures of Hampden.[76] There are no surviving portraits of Winstanley, and until recently the best-known Digger images came from Oscar Zarate's *Winstanley* film poster and from the anarchist illustrator Clifford Harper's imagined portraits of Winstanley.[77] In recent years, however, one of the most famous portraits of Hampden has begun to be linked to Winstanley. On websites, image databases and even on Facebook the portrait is said to be of Winstanley, and it is the standard 'original' image of Winstanley to which picture researchers are often now directed. This has aroused few comments, which is perhaps unsurprising given that Hampden, unlike Winstanley, is little remembered today, at least on this side of the Atlantic.

One place that has been slow to exploit its links with Winstanley is St George's Hill in Surrey, where Diggers are perhaps as unwelcome today as they were in 1649. The hill remained open land for more than two centuries after the Diggers had occupied it, and it became known as 'one of the most picturesque resorts of the public in Surrey'; in Victorian times it was recommended as a place of recreation, and potential visitors were occasionally reminded of the activities of the '"Fifth Monarchy Men", or fanatics of a kindred kind', who had once 'endeavoured to entrench themselves, and live under the new law'.[78] By 1912 the land had been sold by the Egerton family to the builder W.G. Tarrant, and newspapers were soon reporting that the 'beautiful and romantic woods around Cobham' were being destroyed.[79] By the latter part of the century St George's Hill, with its golf course, tennis courts and spectacularly large houses, had become one of the most exclusive private estates near London, and the home to many pop, film and television stars and footballers. Most of the uninvited visitors who now manage to get past the gates and security guards are there to seek out John Lennon's former home, but those curious about Winstanley and the Diggers continue to come too – not only in the occasional well-publicised trespasses but also in many more understated private visits.[80] Although the 'history' sections of the Residents' Association and Golf Club websites go back no further than 1912, the spirit of Winstanley continues to haunt St George's Hill. When squatters took over a derelict mansion on the estate in 2011, they apparently made no connection between their activities and the Diggers, stating innocently and disarmingly that they had 'found the place on Google maps', but the many bloggers who picked up on the story inevitably did make the connection – most likely the hill's residents and management company did so too.[81] We do not know how future generations will regard the Diggers, and whether Winstanley will retain his current, exalted place in the radical and revolutionary tradition. But, for the moment at least, the words of Leon Rosselson's song (in the most optimistic of its many versions) hold good: the Diggers 'were dispersed – but still the vision lingers on'.[82]

A Note on Sources
and Further Reading

I have written in greater detail about the Digger communities and their local context in *Brave Community: The Digger Movement in the English Revolution* (Manchester: Manchester University Press, 2007), and readers wanting to find out more about Winstanley's fellow Diggers and about the local background to the Digger movement may wish to consult that book. In quoting from Winstanley I have made use wherever possible of original seventeenth-century editions. I have however ensured that all endnote references are, for the convenience of readers, to the new and definitive *The Complete Works of Gerrard Winstanley*, 2 vols, ed. Thomas N. Corns, Ann Hughes and David Loewenstein (Oxford: Oxford University Press, 2009), which supersedes all previous collections of Winstanley's works. Readers seeking a shorter and more accessible recent selection from Winstanley's writings will also find much of interest in Tony Benn presents *Gerrard Winstanley: A Common Treasury* (London: Verso, 2011).

Notes

CHAPTER 1

1. Richard Stites, 'Iconoclastic currents in the Russian Revolution: destroying and preserving the past', in Abbott Gleason and Richard Stites (eds.), *Bolshevik Culture: Experiment and Order in the Russian Revolution* (Bloomington: Indiana University Press, 1989), p. 23; Graeme Gill, *Symbols and Legitimacy in Soviet Politics* (Cambridge: Cambridge University Press, 2011), p. 62.
2. *Northern Star*, 22 August 1840, 10 September 1842.
3. The suggestion that Marx was actually referring to Diggers when he spoke of Levellers comes from modern editors of his *Collected Works*.
4. Eduard Bernstein, *Kommunistische und Demokratisch-Sozialistische Ströhmungen während der Englischen Revolution des 17. Jahrhunderts*, in Karl Kautsky (ed.), *Die Vorläufer des neueren Sozialismus: von Thomas More bis zum Vorabend der Französischen Revolution* (Band I, Theil 2 of E. Bernstein, C. Hugo, K. Kautsky, P. Lafargue, F. Mehring and G. Plekhanov, *Die Geschichte des Sozialismus in Einzeldarstellungen*) (Stuttgart: Dietz, 1895), pp. 594–608.
5. For parallels between Winstanley and Marx, see especially James Holstun's 'Communism, George Hill and the *Mir*: was Marx a nineteenth-century Winstanleyan?', in Andrew Bradstock (ed.), *Winstanley and the Diggers, 1649–1999* (London: Frank Cass, 2000), pp. 121–49.
6. Cf. Marx's 'complete restoration of man to himself as a social, i.e. human being', and 'the emancipation of the workers contains universal human emancipation', both from the 1844 'Economic-Philosophical Manuscripts'.
7. Bernstein, *Ströhmungen*, p. 599; Georgi Plekhanov, *Selected Philosophical Works* (Moscow: Progress Publishers, 1976), vol. 3, p. 551.
8. Bernstein, *Ströhmungen*, p. 607.

9. *The Complete Works of Gerrard Winstanley*, ed. Thomas N. Corns, Ann Hughes, and David Loewenstein (Oxford: Oxford University Press, 2009) (hereafter *Works*), vol. 2, p. 80.

10. J. Morrison Davidson, *Concerning Four Precursors of Henry George and the Single Tax as also the Land Gospel according to Winstanley 'The Digger'* (London and Glasgow: Labour Leader Publishing Dept, 1899), p. 93.

11. George Woodcock, *Anarchy or Chaos* (London: Freedom Press, 1944), pp. 27–31.

12. George Orwell, 'Back to the land', *Observer*, 3 September 1944.

13. See, for instance, John Adamson, 'Cavaliers v roundheads continued', *Daily Telegraph*, 21 November 2001.

14. I owe this point to Professor William Lamont, who was a student at the University of London in the 1950s.

15. Perez Zagorin, *A History of Political Thought in the English Revolution* (London: Routledge & Kegan Paul, 1954), pp. 43, 56; G.M. Trevelyan, 'A Puritan Henry George', *Independent Review*, 12 (1907), 338, 339.

16. Recent research on early modern radicalism rightly emphasises the importance of context: see the contributions to Glenn Burgess and Matthew Festenstein (eds.), *English Radicalism, 1550–1850* (Cambridge: Cambridge University Press, 2007); Ariel Hessayon and David Finnegan (eds.), *Varieties of Seventeenth- and Early Eighteenth-Century English Radicalism in Context* (Farnham: Ashgate, 2011); Cromohs Virtual Seminars: 'Radicalism and the English Revolution', www.cromohs.unifi.it/seminari. For the continuing usefulness of the word radical, see Andrew Bradstock, *Radical Religion in Cromwell's England* (London: I.B. Tauris, 2011), pp. xxiii–xxv; Edward Vallance, *A Radical History of Britain* (London: Little, Brown, 2009), pp. 11–18.

17. For the historiography of the English Revolution see especially R.C. Richardson, *The Debate on the English Revolution* (3rd edition, Manchester: Manchester University Press, 1998) and Blair Worden, *Roundhead Reputations: The English Civil Wars and the Passions of Posterity* (London: Allen Lane, 2001).

18. His interpretation of England's bourgeois revolution differed significantly from that of Marx and Engels, for whom the end date was 1688–89 rather than 1660.

19. Christopher Hill (ed.), *The English Revolution 1640: Three Essays* (London: Lawrence & Wishart Ltd, 1940), p. 100.

20. Christopher Hill, *The World Turned Upside Down: Radical Ideas During the English Revolution* (London: Temple Smith, 1972), pp. 11–13.

21. Christopher Hill, *The World Turned Upside Down* (paperback edition, Harmondsworth: Penguin Books, 1975); *Winstanley: The Law of Freedom and Other Writings*, ed. Christopher Hill (Harmondsworth, Penguin Books, 1973).

22. Isabel Taylor, 'Interview with Leon Rosselson', *Albion Magazine Online*, Summer 2007.

23. Information from Professor William Lamont. Sussex has since rid itself of early modern historians, so there is no danger of this happening again.

24. See below, Chapter 5.

25. See below, Chapter 5.

CHAPTER 2

1. Videos of Wigan Diggers' Festival at www.youtube.com; http://wigangreensocialists.wordpress.com; information from Derek Winstanley.

2. *Works*, 2, pp. 80, 81. The second extract was also quoted on the Digger T-shirts produced by The Land is Ours in 1999 and on banners displayed at the 2007 Heathrow climate camp.

3. Opening speech by Stephen Hall of Wigan Borough Green Socialists at Wigan Diggers' Festival, 10 September 2011: www.youtube.com

4. Festival announcement on Wigan World message board at http://www.lqqk.co.uk, added 16 August 2011.

5. Wigan Archives Service, P/W1; John Gurney, *Brave Community: The Digger Movement in the English Revolution* (Manchester: Manchester University Press, 2007), p. 63. For Winstanley's early life see especially J.D. Alsop, 'A high road to radicalism? Gerrard Winstanley's youth', *The Seventeenth Century*, 9 (1994), 11–24; James D. Alsop, 'Gerrard Winstanley: what do we know of his life?', in Bradstock, *Winstanley and the Diggers*, pp. 19–36; *Works*, 1, pp. 1–12.

6. *The Registers of the Parish Church of Wigan, 1580 to 1625*, ed. J. Arrowsmith (Wigan: Lancashire Parish Register Society, 1899), p. 263.

7. *Victoria History of the County of Lancaster (VCH Lancs)*, vol. 4 (London: Constable, 1911), pp. 69, 70; David Sinclair, *The History of Wigan* (Wigan and London: Wall and Kent & Co., 1882), vol. 1, pp. 32–42, vol. 2, pp. 175–6.

8. Ibid., 2, pp. 10–11; *VCH Lancs*, 4, p. 74.

9. Ibid., p. 74; Sinclair, *Wigan*, 2, pp. 6–9.

10. *VCH Lancs*, 4, pp. 71–3; George T.O. Bridgeman, *The History of the Church and Manor of Wigan*, 3 vols (Manchester: Chetham Society, 1888–9), *passim*.

11. Ibid., 1, vi, pp. 141–79; 2, pp. 204–387; Alsop, 'Winstanley's youth', pp. 16–18.

12. *Works*, 1, p. 2. Cf. Alsop, 'Winstanley's youth', p. 18.

13. I owe this point to Derek Winstanley. At least six Wigan boys were given this name in the years 1608–13, and a seventh in 1618. The name was rarely found in other periods: Arrowsmith, *Wigan Registers*, pp. 69, 71, 74, 83, 86, 103.

14. Lancashire Record Office, QDD/42/F7; DDKE/9/17/19; Bridgeman, *Church and Manor*, 2, p. 291; Fred Holcroft, 'Plague in Wigan', *Past Forward*, 39 (2005), 4.

15. Sinclair, *Wigan*, I, p. 198; 2, pp. 3–9. At least 138 burgesses were eligible to vote in 1628.

16. *The Registers of Wigan, 1626–1675*, transc. Len Marsden, ed. Ken T. Taylor (Lancashire Parish Register Society, 2001), p. 232. Cf. also p. 274.

17. *VCH Lancs*, 4, p. 86: Ethan Shagan, *Popular Politics and the English Reformation* (Cambridge: Cambridge University Press, 2003), p. 265.

18. As Alsop points out, the charges were dismissed: Alsop, 'Winstanley's youth', 12–13.

19. Sinclair, *Wigan*, 1, p. 211; Alfred P. Wadsworth and Julia De Lacy Mann, *The Cotton Trade and Industrial Lancashire, 1600–1780* (Manchester: Manchester University Press, 1931), pp. 5–6, 11, 24, 47, 55–6; Norman Lowe, *The Lancashire Textile Industry in the Sixteenth Century* (Manchester: Chetham Society, 1972), pp. 5–6, 15.

20. Ibid., pp. 58–9; Wadsworth and Mann, *Cotton Trade*, p. 8.

21. Ibid., pp. 55–6.

22. The National Archives (TNA), Prob11/79, 127, 132, 282; J.D. Alsop, 'Mason, Henry', *Oxford Dictionary of National Biography (ODNB)*.

23. TNA, Prob11/79, 127.

24. Guildhall Library (GL), MF316/10, p. 91; Alsop, 'Winstanley's youth', 19. Winstanley's term as apprentice was set for eight years from 25 March 1630.
25. TNA, SP14/104/96; Prob11/254, fols 150–2; GL, MF315/9, p. 11; Alsop, 'Winstanley's youth', pp. 15, 19.
26. GL, MF 351/2 (unfol.), 21 February 1637–8.
27. Alsop, 'What do we know of his life?', pp. 22, 23–4; TNA, Prob11/254, fols 150–52.
28. Alsop, 'Mason', *ODNB*. For Mason and the City's religious community see especially Peter Lake, *The Boxmaker's Revenge* (Manchester: Manchester University Press, 2001), pp. 219–21, 224, 227, 232, 233, 242, 404.
29. Henry Mason, *The Cure of Cares* (1627), pp. 1–2, 19–20, 32–5; Henry Mason, *Contentment in Gods Gifts* (1630), p. 63; Henry Mason, *The Tribunall of the Conscience* (1626), pp. 45, 54, 57.
30. *Works*, 1, pp. 51–3, 567; Alsop, 'What do we know of his life?', p. 24.
31. For this see especially Nicholas Tyacke, *Anti-Calvinists: the Rise of English Arminianism, c1590–1640* (Oxford: Clarendon Press, 1987).
32. See Samuel Hoard (co-written with Henry Mason), *Gods Love to Mankind* (1633); John Davenant, *Animadversions upon a Treatise entitled Gods Love to Mankind* (1641); William Twisse, *The Riches of Gods Love* (1653).
33. Henry Mason, *Christian Humiliation, or, a Treatise of Fasting* (1625), dedication; Mason, *Contentment in Gods Gifts*, pp. 55–6, 88–93, 99–100; Henry Mason, *Hearing and Doing the Ready Way to Blessednesse* (1635), pp. 30–2, 243, 429–33, 463; Mason, *The New Art of Lying* (1634); Henry Mason, *Epicures Fast* (1626).
34. Mason, *Cure of Cares*, pp. 32–5; Mason, *Contentment in Gods Gifts*, pp. 63–77.
35. Ibid., pp. 28–37, 39, 41–6, 50–1, 55–6, 57–8, 67–8.
36. Alsop, 'What do we know of his life?', p. 24.
37. GL, MS 4415/1, fol. 90v; Alsop, 'What do we know of his life?', p. 25.
38. GL, MF 316, vol. 12, p. 6; MS 4415/1, fols 90v, 96v, 100v. For a detailed discussion of Winstanley's business career see J.D. Alsop, 'Ethics in the marketplace: Gerrard Winstanley's London bankruptcy', *Journal of British Studies*, 28 (1989).
39. GL, Ms 10,091/22, fol. 184v.

40. Sidney Young, *The Annals of the Barber-Surgeons of London* (London: Blades, East & Blades, 1890), pp. 218, 343, 369; Gurney, *Brave Community*, p. 68.

41. Henry Betham Robinson, 'St Thomas's Hospital surgeons and the practice of their art in the past', *Saint Thomas's Hospital Reports*, New Series, 28 (1901), pp. 420, 422; London Metropolitan Archives (LMA), HO1/ST/A/067/011; F.G. Parsons, *The History of St Thomas's Hospital*, vol. 2 (London: Methuen, 1934), pp. 70–1.

42. Gurney, *Brave Community*, p. 68.

43. TNA, C6/25/85; Gurney, *Brave Community*, pp. 67–9, 71–3. This was a copyhold or customary estate, held by copy of the court roll of the manor of Ham.

44. For popular agitation 1640–42 see especially Brian Manning, *The English People and the English Revolution* (London: Bookmarks, 1991); Keith Lindley, *Popular Politics and Religion in Civil War London* (Aldershot: Scolar Press, 1997); David Cressy, *England on Edge: Crisis and Revolution, 1640–1642* (Oxford: Oxford University Press, 2006).

45. TNA, C6/44/101.

46. Corporation of London Records Office (CLRO), MCD1/71. Winstanley claimed he was owed £274 1s 6d by Backhouse, taking into account a bond in the penalty of £300. The surviving evidence does not appear to support the contention that he was a victim of fraud in this case.

47. TNA, C9/412/269.

48. TNA, C9/412/269; Alsop, 'Ethics in the marketplace', 100–2, 105, 111. For the timing of the move to Cobham, see Gurney, *Brave Community*, p. 71.

49. *Works*, 2, p. 80.

50. Ibid., I, p. 444.

51. Ibid., pp. 510–11.

52. David Taylor, *Cobham: A History* (Chichester: Phillimore & Co., 2003), pp. 1, 14, 27–8; Gurney, *Brave Community*, pp. 1–3.

53. John Gurney, 'William King, Gerrard Winstanley and Cobham', in Bradstock, *Winstanley and the Diggers*, pp. 43, 45; Gurney, *Brave Community*, pp. 71–2.

54. Cobham Conservation and Heritage Trust *Newsletter*, 15 (2009), p. 3, 16 (2009), p. 10.

55. The traditional view is challenged by Alsop in 'What do we know of his life?', pp. 27–8.

56. Surrey History Centre (SHC), K44/1/9; 4398/1/10; Alsop, 'What do we know of his life?', p. 27.

57. SHC, K44/1/9; Gurney, *Brave Community*, pp. 64, 73–4.

58. The impact of the Civil War on Cobham is assessed in ibid., pp. 31–61.

59. Ibid., pp. 43–4.

60. *Works*, 2, p. 80.

61. Gurney, *Brave Community*, pp. 9–16.

62. Ibid., pp. 16–20.

63. Ibid., pp. 34–8, 45–9.

64. Ibid., pp. 49–53; David Taylor, 'Gerrard Winstanley at Cobham', in Bradstock, *Winstanley and the Diggers*, p. 39.

65. Gurney, *Brave Community*, pp. 50–1.

66. John Gurney, 'Gerrard Winstanley and the Digger movement in Walton and Cobham', *Historical Journal* (*HJ*), 37, 4 (1994), 775–802.

67. *Works*, 2, p. 35.

68. Ibid., p. 35; Gurney, *Brave Community*, pp. 52, 159–60.

69. *Works*, 2, p. 284.

70. Ibid., p. 80.

71. For the covenant, see below p. 32.

72. Alsop, 'What do we know of his life?', pp. 26; Gurney, *Brave Community*, pp. 71, 74.

73. Ibid., pp. 65, 74.

74. On the fate of Church of England in the 1640s see John Morrill, 'The church in England', in John Morrill (ed.), *Reactions to the English Civil War, 1642–1649* (London: Macmillan, 1982), pp. 89–114.

75. See Hill, *World Turned Upside Down*, passim.

76. *Works*, 1, p. 98. Cf. ibid., pp. 55, 314; 2, p. 171.

77. David W. Petegorsky, *Left-Wing Democracy in the English Civil War: A Study of the Social Philosophy of Gerrard Winstanley* (London: Victor Gollancz Ltd, for the Left Book Club, 1940), p. 125. Cf. Andrew Bradstock, *Faith in the Revolution* (London: SPCK, 1997), p. 85, for the difficulties of identifying the source of Winstanley's inspiration at any given time.

78. Alsop, 'What do we know of his life?', p. 20; *Works*, 1, p. 59.

79. I am indebted to Ariel Hessayon for sending me a draft of his unpublished essay on Winstanley and Boehme.

80. *Works*, 1, pp. 51–3.

81. Ibid., p. 449.

82. See especially J.F. McGregor, 'The Baptists: fount of all heresy', in J.F. McGregor and B. Reay (eds.), *Radical Religion in the English Revolution* (Oxford: Oxford University Press, 1984), pp. 23–63; Bradstock, *Radical Religion*, pp. 1–25.

83. Ariel Hessayon, 'Gerrard Winstanley, radical reformer', in Hessayon and Finnegan, *English Radicalism*, pp. 87–112.

84. Thomas Edwards, *Gangraena* (1646), III, pp. 27–30, 51–2; Ann Hughes, *Gangraena and the Struggle for the English Revolution* (Oxford: Oxford University Press (2004), pp. 246–7.

85. Thomas Collier, *Certaine Queries* (1645), pp. 4–5, 24, 27; Thomas Collier, *A Brief Discovery of the Corruption of the Ministrie of the Church of England* (1647), pp, 11–12, 20, 26–7; Thomas Collier, *A Discovery of the New Creation* (1647), pp. 8–9, 13–14, 15, 16–18, 20, 27, 29–30, 31–4; Thomas Collier, *A General Epistle to the Universall Church of the First Born* (1648), pp. 10, 14–15, 46, 48, 50–1, 56, 58, 83–7; Thomas Collier, *A Third General Epistle to the Saints*, in *The Works of Thomas Collier* (1652), pp. 357, 361; Thomas Collier, *The Heads and Substance of a Discourse* (1651), pp. 5–8, 13, 19. Cf. Thomas Hall, *The Collier in his Colours* (1652), pp. 121, 125, 126–7.

86. For instance, Collier, *Discovery of the New Creation*, epistle to the reader, pp. 9, 14; Collier, *General Epistle*, p. 105; Thomas Collier, *A Second Generall Epistle* (1649), pp. 57, 60, 61, 62.

87. John Saltmarsh, *Sparkles of Glory* (1647), pp. 291–2; John Saltmarsh, *Groanes for Liberty* (1646), p. 23.

88. On Seekers, see especially J.F. McGregor, 'Seekers and Ranters', in McGregor and Reay, *Radical Religion*, pp. 121–9.

89. *Works*, 1, pp. 98, 102, 104, 257, 434, 448–9, 486. Cf. ibid., pp. 277, 317, 322–3.

90. Ibid., pp. 69–71.

91. *The Works of Gerrard Winstanley*, ed. George H. Sabine (Ithaca: Cornell University Press, 1941), pp. 79–96; Petegorsky, *Left-Wing Democracy*, pp. 124, 125.

92. *Works*, 1, pp. 101–312.

93. Collier, *Discovery of the New Creation*, dedicatory epistle; pp. 8–9, 14–15. Cf. Collier, *Second Generall Epistle*, p. 57.

94. *Works*, 1, pp. 262–3, 314, 416; Thomas N. Corns, 'The road to George Hill: the heretical dynamic of Winstanley's early prose', in David Loewenstein and John Marshall (eds.), *Heresy*

and Literature in Early Modern English Culture (Cambridge: Cambridge University Press, 2006), p. 193.

95. *Works*, 1, pp. 314–15, 357, 412.
96. Ibid., pp. 375, 413.
97. Collier, *Second Generall Epistle*, pp. 34–5.
98. Saltmarsh, *Sparkles of Glory*, pp. 1–8; Thomas Collier, *The Marrow of Christianity* (1650), dedicatory epistle, pp. 14–17, 29; Collier, *Second Generall Epistle*, p. 35.
99. *Works*, 1, pp. 424, 425–8. Cf. ibid., p. 332.
100. For Winstanley's attitude towards magistracy, see esp. J.C. Davis, *Utopia and the Ideal Society* (Cambridge: Cambridge University Press, 1981), pp. 169–203.
101. Corns, 'Road to George hill', pp. 189–90; *Works*, 1, pp. 69–74.
102. The terms 'Independent' and 'Presbyterian' were applied in the late 1640s to the two main political groupings in parliament, who differed principally over what form of political settlement should be established after the end of the war. These groups were loosely related to, but by no means identical with, the religious Independents and Presbyterians, who disagreed over what form the state church should take after the collapse of the established church.
103. For useful recent accounts of post-war political developments, see Michael Braddick, *God's Fury, England's Fire* (London: Penguin, 2008), pp. 439–550; Mark Kishlansky, *A Monarchy Transformed: Britain 1603–1714* (London: Penguin, 1996), pp. 158–86.
104. Gurney, *Brave Community*, pp. 75–6, 97.
105. *Works*, 1, pp. 102, 166, 281, 285.
106. Gurney, *Brave Community*, p. 76.
107. John Fielder, *The Humble Petition and Appeal of John Fielder* (1651), pp. 1–2, 4–5, 12–22; TNA, SP24/61, Lidgold v Fielder, 1650; L.F. Solt, 'Winstanley, Lilburne and the case of John Fielder', *Huntington Library Quarterly*, 45, 2 (1982), 119–36; Gurney, *Brave Community*, pp. 42, 76–8; *Works*, 1, pp. 435–9.
108. Gurney, *Brave Community*, pp. 77–8.
109. *Works*, 2, pp. 9–10, 38, 54, 72, 85, 88. Cf. Edward Vallance, *Revolutionary England and the National Covenant* (Woodbridge: Boydell & Brewer, 2005), pp. 149–53.
110. For Bickerstaffe see Gurney, 'Digger movement', pp. 782–5; Gurney, *Brave Community*, pp. 4, 32, 36, 96, 128; John Gurney, 'Bickerstaffe, Henry, Digger', *ODNB*.

111. Gurney, 'William King', p. 44; Gurney, 'Digger movement', p. 791; Gurney, *Brave Community*, viii–ix, pp. 73, 132, 166.

112. Ariel Hessayon, 'Everard, William, Digger', *ODNB*.

113. Gurney, *Brave Community*, p. 77; *Works*, 1, p. 412.

114. Hessayon, 'Everard', *ODNB*.

115. Gurney, *Brave Community*, p. 155.

116. *Journal of the House of Commons (CJ)* (1802), vol. 6, p. 111.

117. S.R. Gardiner (ed.), *The Constitutional Documents of the Puritan Revolution, 1625–1660* (Oxford: Oxford University Press, third edition, 1906), pp. 384–8.

118. Blair Worden, *The Rump Parliament* (Cambridge: Cambridge University Press, 1974), esp. pp. 25–7, 33–40, 51–2, 171–4.

119. Brian Manning, *1649: The Crisis of the English Revolution* (London: Bookmarks, 1992), pp. 79–82. Cf. Steve Hindle, 'Dearth and the English revolution: the harvest crisis of 1647–50', *Economic History Review*, 61 (2008).

120. *A True Representation of the Present Sad and Lamentable Condition of the County of Lancaster* (1649); Gurney, *Brave Community*, p. 111.

121. J.C. Davis and J.D.Alsop, 'Winstanley, Gerrard', *ODNB*; Alsop, 'What do we know of his life?', p. 28.

122. Richard Overton, *Certaine Queries*, in his *An Appeale from the Degenerate Representative Body* (1647), p. 38. Cf. *The Case of the Armie Truly Stated* (1647), p. 19; *Englands Troublers Troubled* (1648), pp. 7–8; *To the Honourable, the Supreame Authority of this Nation* (1649); *The Humble Petition of Divers Inhabitants of the City of London and Parts Adjacent* (1649), p. 7; *A Declaration of the Armie concerning Lieut. Collonel John Lilburn* (1651), p. 4.

123. *Light Shining in Buckinghamshire* (1648), pp. 1–2, 7.

124. Ibid., p. 5.

125. *A Declaration of the Wel-Affected in the County of Buckinghamshire* (1649), p. 8.

126. *Works*, 1, pp. 473, 480, 485, 486, 494, 495, 496–9.

127. Collier, *Second Generall Epistle*, pp. 57, 60–3, 76.

128. *Works*, 1, pp. 476, 477, 480.

129. Ibid., p. 481.

130. Ibid., pp. 481, 482.

131. Ibid., pp. 504, 505, 506, 511, 519, 523.

132. Ibid., pp. 507, 509, 522.

133. Ibid., pp. 486, 508, 523–4, 553. Cf. G.E. Aylmer, 'The religion of Gerrard Winstanley', in McGregor and Reay, *Radical Religion*, pp. 92–3.
134. *Works*, 1, pp. 508, 516; Collier, *Second General Epistle*, p. 76.
135. *Works*, 1, pp. 514, 517.
136. Ibid., pp. 504, 514, 519, 534, 535.
137. Ibid., pp. 507–8, 520–1. Cf. Davis, *Utopia*, p. 180.
138. *Works*, 1, pp. 513, 516–17, 523.
139. Ibid., p. 524.

CHAPTER 3

1. From the preface to *A Watch-Word to the City of London* (1649), in *Works*, 2, p. 80.
2. 8 April has sometimes been suggested as the start date, but 1 April is confirmed in Digger writings and legal records: Winstanley, *Works*, 2, p. 146; John Coulton, *Theoria Contingentium Anni Aerae Christianae 1653* (1653); TNA, ASSI 35/91/4.
3. SHC, 44/1/9.
4. *Works*, 2, pp. 4, 5.
5. Ibid., pp. 6, 7.
6. Ibid., pp. 10, 19.
7. Ibid., pp. 10, 11–12, 13, 14–15, 16.
8. Ibid., pp. 4, 5, 8, 12, 16–17, 18.
9. Ibid., pp. 8, 9, 17.
10. The classic study is Christopher Hill, 'The Norman yoke', in his *Puritanism and Revolution* (Harmondsworth: Penguin Books, 1986), pp. 58–125.
11. *Works*, 2, pp. 12, 13.
12. Cf. Hill, 'Norman yoke', p. 87.
13. *More Light Shining in Buckinghamshire* (1649), pp. 13–16.
14. *Works*, 2, pp. 9, 10, 13.
15. For the languages of early modern social protest, see especially Andy Wood, *The 1549 Rebellions and the Making of Early Modern England* (Cambridge: Cambridge University Press, 2007), pp. 7–8, 91–104; Steve Hindle, 'Imagining insurrection in seventeenth-century England: representations of the Midland rising of 1607', *History Workshop Journal*, 66 (2008), 21–9, 48.
16. *More Light Shining*, pp. 4, 9, 13.

17. *A Declaration or Representation of ... divers of the Inhabitants of the County of Hartford* (1649/50), pp. 3–5, 7.

18. Gurney, *Brave Community*, pp. 128–34; Gurney, 'Winstanley and the Digger movement', 781–5, 790–4; Winstanley, *Works*, 2, pp. 441–56. See also David Mulder, *The Alchemy of Revolution: Gerrard Winstanley's Occultism and Seventeenth-Century English Communism* (New York: Lang, 1990), pp. 304–31.

19. For the suggestion that some support was organised through Calvert's London bookshop, see Mario Carrichio, '*News from the New Jerusalem*: Giles Calvert and the radical experience', in Hessayon and Finnegan, *English Radicalism*, p. 69.

20. *The Clarke Papers*, ed. C.H. Firth, vol. 2 (London: Camden Society, 1894), p. 210.

21. Owen Manning and William Bray, *The History and Antiquities of the County of Surrey* (London: J. White, 1804–14), vol. 2, p. 758; John Nichols (ed.), *Illustrations of the Literary History of the Eighteenth Century*, vol. 4 (London: printed for the author, 1822), p. 502.

22. Gurney, *Brave Community*, pp. 137–42; Alun Howkins, 'From Diggers to Dongas: the land in English radicalism, 1649–2000', *History Workshop Journal*, 54 (2002), 21.

23. *Clarke Papers*, 2, pp. 210–11.

24. Ibid., p. 211; Gurney, *Brave Community*, pp. 121–2, 137–8.

25. *Works*, p. 146. For Taylor see John Gurney, '"Furious divells"?: the Diggers and their opponents', in Bradstock, *Winstanley and the Diggers*, pp. 75–6; Gurney, *Brave Community*, pp. 155–6, 175.

26. TNA, SP25/94, pp. 93, 94; *Clarke Papers*, 2, pp. 209–10.

27. Ibid., pp. 211–12.

28. *Perfect Diurnall* (16–23 April 1649), p. 2450.

29. *The Declaration and Standard of the Levellers of England* (1649). Cf. *Modest Narrative of Intelligence*, 3 (14–21 April 1649).

30. *Moderate*, 41 (17–24 April); *Kingdomes Faithfull and Impartiall Scout* (20–27 April 1649). Cf. *Perfect Summary of an Exact Diarie* (16–23 April); *Mercurius Pragmaticus (for Charles II)* (17–24 April); *Kingdomes Weekly Intelligencer*, 308 (17–24 April); *Moderate Intelligencer*, 214 (19–26 April 1649).

31. *Man in the Moon*, 4 (April–May); *Mercurius Pragmaticus* (17–23 April); *Perfect Occurences*, 120 (13–20 April 1649).

32. *Perfect Summary* (23–30 April); *Modest Narrative* (21–28 April 1649); British Library (BL), Add. MS 37,344, fol. 286.

33. *Perfect Summary* (16–23 April); *Moderate Intelligencer*, 214 (19–26 April); *Kingdomes Faithfull and Impartiall Scout* (20–27 April 1649).

34. *Mercurius Pramaticus* (17–24 April 1649). Cf. *Man in the Moon*, 4; *Declaration and Standard*.

35. On Pordage see especially Manfred Brod, 'A radical network in the English revolution: John Pordage and his circle, 1646–54', *English Historical Review*, 119, 484 (2004), 1230–53.

36. John Pordage, *Innocence Appearing through the Dark Mists of Pretended Guilt* (1651), pp. 72–3; Richard Baxter, *Reliquiae Baxterianae*, ed. Matthew Sylvester (1696), pp. 77–8.

37. Hessayon, 'Everard', *ODNB*.

38. The London bookseller George Thomason dated his copy 26 April.

39. *Works*, 2, pp. 140, 144, 145. This usage was quite common in radical discourse: for God as 'mighty Leveller' see Abiezer Coppe, *A Fiery-Flying Roll* (1649), pp. 2, 6; George Foster, *The Sounding of the Last Trumpet* (1650), p. 14. Both knew Winstanley's writings.

40. *Modest Narrative of Intelligence* (21–28 April 1649).

41. For instance in Hill, *Law of Freedom*, pp. 75–95.

42. John Lilburne, Thomas Prince and Richard Overton, *The Picture of the Councel of State* (1649), pp. 14–15.

43. S.R. Gardiner, *History of the Commonwealth and Protectorate*, vol. 1 (London: Longmans, Green & Co., 1903 edition), pp. 44–54; Ian Gentles, *The New Model Army in England, Ireland and Scotland, 1645–1653* (Oxford: Blackwell Publishers, 1992), pp. 315–49; Manning, *1649*, pp. 201–6; Brian Manning, *The Far Left in the English Revolution, 1640 to 1660* (London: Bookmarks, 1999), pp. 81–111. Gentles estimates that as many as 2,500 soldiers were involved in mutinies in the spring and summer of 1649. For the concept of 'physical force Levellerism' see Hill, *World Turned Upside Down*, pp. 91–2; Manning, *Far Left*, pp. 89–91.

44. Petegorsky, *Left-Wing Democracy*, pp. 167–8; Olivier Lutaud, *Winstanley: Socialisme et Christianisme sous Cromwell* (Paris: Didier, 1976), p. 178. It is usually assumed that he was mistaken for Robert Everard, who was certainly involved in the mutinies.

45. TNA, SP28/94, p. 94.

46. [John Canne], *The Discoverer*, part I (1649), pp. 8–9, 12–14. Cf. [John Canne], *Lieut. Colonel John Lilb. Tryed and Cast* (1653), pp. 84, 86–7.

47. *Perfect Occurences*, 126 (25 May–1 June 1649), p. 1053. These were apparently the journalist's words, rather than – as is often assumed – Cromwell's.

48. H[umphey] B[rooke], *The Crafts-mens Craft* (1649), pp. 5–6.

49. John Lilburne, *Legal Fundamental Liberties* (1649), p. 75.

50. John Lilburne, *L. Colonel John Lilburne his Apologetical Narration* (1652), pp. 68–9; G.E. Aylmer (ed.), *The Levellers in the English Revolution* (London: Thames & Hudson, 1975), pp. 87, 153–4; *The Writings of William Walwyn*, ed. Jack R. McMichael and Barbara Taft (Athens: University of Georgia Press, 1989), pp. 42, 49, 80; Brooke, *Crafts-mens Craft*, pp. 8–9; A.L. Morton, *The World of the Ranters: Religious Radicalism in the English Revolution* (London: Lawrence & Wishart, 1970), pp. 183–7; Manning, *Far Left*, pp. 51–2.

51. Brian Manning, review of Bradstock, *Winstanley and the Diggers*, *Historical Materialism*, 13, 3 (2005), 238.

52. For the earliest use of the name see Worden, *Roundhead Reputations*, pp. 318–19.

53. Cf. Petegorsky, *Left-Wing Democracy*, p. 111.

54. For example Hill, *1640*, pp. 67–8, 69; A.L. Morton, *The Story of the English Revolution* (London: Communist Party, 1949), p. 13. Cf. Worden, *Roundhead Reputations*, p. 335; below, Chapter 5.

55. Christopher Hill and Edmund Dell (eds.), *The Good Old Cause* (London: Lawrence & Wishart, 1949), p. 401.

56. For instance, Manning, *English People*, pp. 358–424; Norah Carlin, *The First English Revolution* (London: Socialist Workers Party 1983), pp. 21–5, 41.

57. *Works*, 1, pp. 79–82. This is the title preferred in the 2009 OUP edition of Winstanley's *Complete Works*.

58. For early use of the Digger name see *Moderate*, 41 (17–24 April); *Kingdomes Faithfull and Impartiall Scout* (20–27 April 1649). Winstanley was using the name by June at the latest.

59. Steve Hindle, 'Imagining insurrection', 21.

60. *A Declaration of the Wel-affected in the County of Buckinghamshire* (1649), p. 8; Gurney, *Brave Community*, pp. 135–7.

61. *Works*, 2, pp. 33, 36–9.

62. Gurney, *Brave Community*, pp. 142–3.

63. Ibid., pp. 157–9; *Works*, 2, p. 69. Cf. ibid., p. 48, 89.

64. Ibid., pp. 43–55; *The Speeches of the Lord Generall Fairfax, and the Other Officers of the Armie, to the Diggers at St Georges Hill in Surrey* (1649).

65. *Mercurius Republicus* (22–29 May 1649); *Works*, 2, p. 146.

66. Ibid., p. 47.

67. Gurney, *Brave Community*, p. 156.

68. *Works*, 2, pp. 59, 60.

69. Gurney, '"Furious divells"?', pp. 75–7; Gurney, *Brave Community*, pp. 155–7.

70. [John Hart], *Trodden Down in Strength* (1647); Gurney, *Brave Community*, pp. 161–2.

71. J.T. Rutt (ed.), *Diary of Thomas Burton Esq* (London: H. Colburn, 1828), vol. 1, pp. 55–6, 107.

72. Kingston Museum and Heritage Service (KMHS), KE1/1/14; *Works*, 2, pp. 82–4; Gurney, *Brave Community*, pp. 162–3.

73. *Works*, 2, pp. 90, 96. 'Mr Gilder' was George Gildon of Kingston.

74. Ibid., pp. 92, 96, 97.

75. Ibid., pp. 80, 93, 95, 96, 97. Cf. Nigel Smith, 'Gerrard Winstanley and the literature of revolution', in Bradstock, *Winstanley and the Diggers*, pp. 48–51.

76. *Works*, 2, pp. 93, 96–7.

77. Ibid., pp. 79, 81, 86–7. Cf. Christopher Hill, 'Winstanley and freedom', in R.C. Richardson and G.M. Ridden (eds.), *Freedom and the English Revolution* (Manchester: Manchester University Press, 1986), pp. 151–68; Gurney, *Brave Community*, pp. 163–5.

78. *Works*, 2, pp. 108–21.

79. Ibid., pp. 107–234; Keith Thomas, 'The date of Gerrard Winstanley's *Fire in the Bush*', *Past & Present* (*P&P*), 42 (1969), 160–2; Aylmer, 'Religion of Gerrard Winstanley', pp. 105–8; Gurney, *Brave Community*, pp. 176–9.

80. This is backed up by surviving evidence of who was involved in attacks on the Diggers. Patterns of opposition in Cobham are discussed in ibid., pp. 167–74, 176, 192–3; Gurney, 'Digger movement', 785–8.

81. BL, Egerton MS 2618, fol. 38; TNA, SP25/94, pp. 477–8; *Brief Relation*, 3 (16 October); *Mercurius Elenticus*, 25 (15–22 October 1649).

82. KMHS, KE1/1/14, pp. 328, 336, 338; *Works*, 1, intro, p. 34; 2, p. 115; Gurney, *Brave Community*, p. 167.

83. Ibid., pp. 76, 139, 167–8; *Works*, 2, pp. 117, 413, 416–7.

84. Ibid., pp. 120, 122, 147, 412.

85. Ibid., p. 123. Cf. ibid., pp. 149, 412–13.

86. Ibid., pp. 122–3.

87. Ibid., pp. 123–4. Cf. ibid., p. 147.

88. Ibid., pp. 129, 145, 147, 149.

89. Ibid., p. 149. Cf. ibid., pp. 411–13.

90. Ibid., pp. 132, 133, 143.

91. *Speeches of the Lord Generall Fairfax*; Gurney, '"Furious divells"?', pp. 82–3; Gurney, *Brave Community*, pp. 190–1.

92. Ibid., p. 191; *Works*, 2, pp. 118, 119. Cf. ibid., pp. 192–3, 196, 218–19.

93. Ibid., p. 413. Cf. ibid., p. 149.

94. Keith Thomas, 'Another Digger broadside', *P&P*, 42 (1969), 57–68; Hill, *World Turned Upside Down*, pp. 99–101; Gurney, *Brave Community*, pp. 185–91.

95. Ibid., pp. 166, 175–6; Sabine, *Works*, pp. 653–75.

96. Ibid., pp. 203–4; Gurney, *Brave Community*, pp. 181–4.

97. Ibid., pp. 124, 179–80.

98. *Records of the Churches of Christ, gathered at Fenstanton, Warboys, and Hexham, 1644–1720*, ed. Edward Bean Underhill (London: Hansard Knollys Society, 1854), pp. 269–71. Cf. Hill, *World Turned Upside Down*, p. 102.

99. Thomas Comber, *Christianity no Enthusiasm* (1678), pp. 90–2, 181; Thomas Tenison, *An Argument for Union* (1683), pp. 8–9; Thomas Tenison, *A Discourse concerning a Guide in Matters of Faith* (1683), p. 31; Lewis H. Berens, *The Digger Movement in the Days of the Commonwealth* (London: Simpkin, Marshall, Hamilton, Kent, & Co. Ltd, 1906), pp. 47–67. Cf. *Works*, 1, p. 71.

100. Winthrop S. Hudson, 'Gerrard Winstanley and the early Quakers', *Church History*, 12, 3 (1943).

101. William C. Braithwaite, *The Second Period of Quakerism*, 2nd edition, ed. Henry J. Cadbury (Cambridge: Cambridge University Press, 1955), pp. 556–7.

102. For example Petegorsky, *Left-Wing Democracy*, p. 248; Hill and Dell, *Good Old Cause*, p. 401; Hill, *Law of Freedom*, p. 33.

103. George Fox, *The Journal*, ed. Nigel Smith (London: Penguin Books, 1998), pp. 7, 11, 45; 57, 141–2, 147, 149.

104. See the entries for Stephens in the *DNB* and *ODNB*; Hill, *World Turned Upside Down*, p. 102, n. 92.

105. Nathaniel Stephens, *A Plain and Easie Calculation of the Name, Mark and Number of the Name of the Beast* (1656), pp. 267–70. Cf. *Works*, 2, p. 196.

106. George Fox, *A Declaration Against all Profession and Professors* (1654), pp. 4, 7, 10, 11, 12; George Fox, *Newes Coming Up Out of the North* (1653); George Fox, *The Vials of the Wrath of God* (1654), pp. 5, 11–12.

107. Barry Reay, 'Quaker opposition to tithes, 1652–1660', *P&P*, 86 (1980), 98–120; Barry Reay, 'Quakerism and society', in McGregor and Reay, *Radical Religion*, pp. 149–51; Rosemary Moore, *The Light in their Consciences: The Early Quakers in Britain, 1646–1666* (University Park, PA: Pennsylvania State University Press, 2000), pp. 63–6.

108. Fox, *Declaration*, p. 12; Reay, 'Quakerism', p. 151.

109. *Works*, 2, p. 44.

110. For an important recent survey of Winstanley and his possible influence over the Quakers see David Boulton, *Gerrard Winstanley and the Republic of Heaven* (Dent: Dales Historical Monographs, 1999).

111. *Works*, 2, pp. 430–1.

112. Ibid., pp. 295–6.

113. Ibid., p. 433.

114. Gardiner, *Constitutional Documents*, p. 391.

115. Quentin Skinner, 'History and ideology in the English revolution', *HJ*, 8 (1965), 151–78; Quentin Skinner, 'Conquest and consent: Thomas Hobbes and the engagement controversy', in G.E. Aylmer (ed.), *The Interregnum: The Quest for Settlement, 1646–1660* (London: Macmillan, 1972), pp. 79–98.

116. G.E. Aylmer, '*England's Spirit Unfoulded, Or an Incouragement to take the Engagement*: a newly discovered pamphlet by Gerrard Winstanley', *P&P*, 40 (1968), 3–15; *Works*, 2, pp. 161–7. Cf. ibid., pp. 211, 265–6.

117. Hampshire Record Office, 44M69/A6/3/1, p.13; Gurney, *Brave Community*, pp. 174–5.

118. *Works*, 2, pp. 244, 247, 248–9.

119. Ibid., pp. 244, 256, 258.

120. Gurney, *Brave Community*, p. 193.

121. *Works*, 2, pp. 119, 121–2, 167, 209, 235–40, 431–2.

122. Ibid., p. 268.

123. Gurney, 'Digger movement', 788–90; Gurney, *Brave Community*, pp. 171–4, 193–5.

124. *Works*, 2, pp. 268, 269, 270–1.
125. Ibid., pp. 269, 271.
126. Thomas, 'Another Digger broadside', 65.
127. Gurney, 'Digger movement', 788–9; Gurney, *Brave Community*, pp. 171, 185, 190, 210.
128. *Works*, 2, pp. 267, 269.
129. Francis Higginson, *A Brief Relation of the Irreligion of the Northern Quakers* (1653), p. 27.
130. Reay, 'Quakerism and society', p. 149 n. 36.

CHAPTER 4

1. *Works*, 2, pp. 287–8.
2. Gurney, *Brave Community*, p. 211.
3. For her career and writings see Esther S. Cope, *Handmaid of the Holy Spirit: Dame Eleanor Davies, Never Soe Mad a Ladie* (Ann Arbor: University of Michigan Press, 1992); *Prophetic Writings of Lady Eleanor Davies*, ed. Esther S. Cope (New York: Oxford University Press, 1995).
4. *Works*, 2, pp. 422–3, 425. By sequestration he probably meant the seizure of corn and goods by court order in 1650: Cope, *Handmaid*, p. 156.
5. Hill, *Law of Freedom*, p. 31; Nigel Smith (ed.), *A Collection of Ranter Writings* (London: Junction Books, 1983), p. 182.
6. A.L. Rowse, *Reflections on the Puritan Revolution* (London: Methuen, 1986), pp. 211–12.
7. Cope, *Handmaid*, p. 156.
8. *Works*, 2, pp. 422–5.
9. Ibid., pp. 302, 359–63, 374.
10. Ibid., pp. 292–3, 294, 302, 315, 321, 322, 359, 371.
11. Ibid., pp. 317–20, 334–5, 350, 353.
12. Ibid., pp. 340–1, 342, 370.
13. Ibid., pp. 342, 354–5, 377.
14. Ibid., pp. 294, 295–6, 302, 304–14, 366–75.
15. Bernstein, *Ströhmungen*, pp. 594–608.
16. *Works*, 1, p. 485; 2, p. 4. Cf. Christopher Hill, *A Nation of Change and Novelty: Religion and Literature in Seventeenth-Century England* (London: Routledge, 1990), pp. 122–3.

17. *Works*, 2, pp. 312–13, 315, 320, 321, 322, 326, 334, 357, 378; Elaine Hobby, 'Winstanley, women and the family', in Bradstock, *Winstanley and the Diggers*, pp. 61–72.

18. *Works*, 1, pp. 47–8; Ann Hughes, *Gender and the English Revolution* (London: Routledge, 2012), pp. 116–18. Cf. Hobby, 'Winstanley, women and the family', p. 70.

19. Phyllis Mack, 'The prophet and her audience: gender and knowledge in The World Turned Upside Down', in Geoff Eley and William Hunt (eds.), *Reviving the English Revolution: Reflections and Elaborations on the Work of Christopher Hill* (London: Verso, 1988), pp. 143–4. Though see also James Holstun, *Ehud's Dagger: Class Struggle in the English Revolution* (London: Verso, 2000), pp. 426–8, for a slightly more favourable assessment.

20. *Works*, 2, pp. 315–42, 348–63, 366–79.

21. Ibid., pp. 321, 331, 369–78. The death penalty would apply to those guilty of buying and selling, preaching for hire, practising law for money, and rape.

22. Ibid., p. 45; *Works*, 1, pp. 515, 523.

23. Edmund Dell, 'Gerrard Winstanley and the Diggers', *Modern Quarterly*, NS, 4, 2 (1949), 138–9.

24. Marie Louise Berneri, *Journey Through Utopia* (London: Freedom Press, 1950), pp. 170, 172; Peter Marshall, *Demanding the Impossible: A History of Anarchism* (London: Fontana Press, 1992), pp. 100–1.

25. *Works*, 2, pp. 220, 354. The two passages are not necessarily contradictory: see W. Schenk, *The Concern for Social Justice in the Puritan Revolution* (London: Longmans, Green and Co., 1948), p. 108.

26. *Works*, 2, p. 296.

27. *Works*, 1, pp. 508, 514–15, 520; above, Chapter 2. Cf. Davis, *Utopia*, p. 180.

28. *Works*, 2, pp. 83, 198. Cf. Davis, *Utopia*, pp. 181–2, 182–3.

29. *Works*, 2, pp. 294, 305–6, 308, 311–12, 348. Cf. Bradstock, *Faith in the Revolution*, pp. 90–2; Gurney, *Brave Community*, p. 213.

30. *Works*, 2, pp. 280, 288, 306, 308.

31. For Winstanley and Hobbes, see esp. Hill, *World Turned Upside Down*, pp. 313–19.

32. Cf. Worden, *Rump Parliament*, pp. 272, 274–5, 279.

33. Penington's influence is discussed in John Gurney, 'Gerrard Winstanley's *The Law of Freedom*: context and continuity', in J.C. Davis and M.A. Ramiro (eds.), *Utopian Moments: Reading Utopian Texts* (London: Bloomsbury Academic, 2012), pp. 47–52.

34. Canne, *Lieut. Colonel John Lilb.*, pp. 39–40.

35. See their statement to this effect in their *A Manifestation* (1649), in Aylmer, *Levellers*, pp. 156–7.

36. *Works*, 2, pp. 317, 318–21, 340–1, 368.

37. Gurney, '*Law of Freedom*', pp. 49, 51–2.

38. Berens, *Digger Movement*, p. 232; Petegorsky, *Left-Wing Democracy*, p. 232; Austin Woolrych, *Commonwealth to Protectorate* (Oxford: Clarendon Press, 1982), p. 39.

39. *A Declaration of the Commoners of England, to his Excellency The Lord General Cromwell* (1652); *Articles of High Treason* (1652); *A New Way to Pay Old Debts: Or, The Law and Freedom of the People Established* (1652); *Faithful Scout*, 56 (6–13 Feb.), 439; 58 (20–27 February), 454–5; *French Intelligencer* (4–11 February), 87; (11–18 February 1652), 90.

40. *Works*, 2, p. 359.

41. *The Levellers New Remonstrance or Declaration* (1649), pp. 1–3, 6; *The King of Scots Declaration* (1649), pp. 4–5. Cf. *Englands Moderate Messenger* (12–19 June 1649), 58–60. Cf. *Works*, 2, p. 55, n.1.

42. *Faithful Scout*, 66 (16–23 April 1652), 518–19; Gurney, *Brave Community*, p. 216.

43. *Works*, 1, pp. 16, 23; Alsop, 'What do we know of his life?', pp. 30–2.

44. Gurney, *Brave Community*, p. 211.

45. See above, p. 85.

46. He served for a second time as waywarden in 1666.

47. Bill Stevenson, 'The social integration of post-restoration dissenters, 1660–1725', in Margaret Spufford (ed.), *The World of the Rural Dissenters* (Cambridge: Cambridge University Press, 1995), pp. 360–87. For Carter, see Gurney, *Brave Community*, p. 219.

48. Ibid., p. 218; *Works*, 1, p. 19.

49. KMHS, KE2/7/2, 7, 10, 12.

50. For the fate of Platt and other Surrey ministers see David L. Wykes, 'Early religious dissent in Surrey after the Restoration', *Southern History*, 33 (2011), 54–77.

51. Gurney, 'Bickerstaffe', *ODNB*.

52. Gurney, 'Digger movement', 790–1.

53. Joseph Besse, *A Collection of the Sufferings of People called Quakers*, vol. 1 (London, 1753), p. 698.

54. TNA, C9/412/269; C6/44/101; C5/415/123; C24/867/102; Alsop, 'Ethics in the marketplace', 100–2, 109–12; R.J. Dalton, 'Gerrard Winstanley: the experience of fraud', *HJ*, 34, 4 (1991), 975.

55. TNA C9/412/269; C24/867/102; Gurney, *Brave Community*, pp. 65, 220.

56. For his career and contacts see ibid., pp. 64–5, 139, 187, 220, corrected (for his date of birth) by John Le Neve, *Monumenta Anglicana* (1719), pp. 67–8.

57. CLRO, MC1/83/232; Dalton, 'Experience of fraud', 979–80; Gurney, *Brave Community*, pp. 68, 73, 216–17.

58. TNA, C6/25/85; C6/26/73; Prob11/320, fols 103–4; Gurney, *Brave Community*, pp. 69, 71, 217–18.

59. TNA, C5/413/199; C6/25/85; C6/26/73; Gurney, *Brave Community*, p. 217.

60. TNA, C6/25/85; Prob11/320, fols 103–4; James D. Alsop, 'Gerrard Winstanley's later life', *P&P*, 82 (1979), 75.

61. Gurney, *Brave Community*, pp. 65, 219.

62. These actions are described in Richard T. Vann, 'The later life of Gerrard Winstanley', *Journal of the History of Ideas*, 26 (1965), 135; Alsop, 'Later life', 74, 77–9; Gurney, *Brave Community*, pp. 219–20. The most detailed account is in *Works*, 1, pp. 19–23.

63. TNA, Prob11/316, fols 398v ff.

64. Thomas Lord Coningsby, *The Case of the Right Honourable Thomas Earl Coningesby* (1722), pp. 78, 79, 80, 82, 84, 85.

65. For Coningsby's reputation see Pat Rogers, *The Life and Times of Thomas Lord Coningsby: the Whig Hangman and his Victims* (London: Continuum, 2011), p. 2.

66. Hill's narrative is in *A Brief Narrative of that Stupendious Tragedie* (1662). For details of the plot see Richard L. Greaves, *Deliver Us from Evil: The Radical Underground in Britain, 1660–1663* (New York: Oxford University Press, 1986), pp. 109–34.

67. TNA, C6/188/19, 66, 67; C6/192/31.

68. TNA, C5/581/55; C6/244/96; *Works*, 1, pp. 21–3; Vann, 'Later life', 135; Alsop, 'Later life', 78–9.

69. TNA, RG6/827, p. 21; Vann, 'Later life', 135; Alsop, 'Later life', 80–1; Gurney, *Brave Community*, pp. 220–1.

70. TNA, RG6/825, p. 19; Gurney, *Brave Community*, p. 221.

71. TNA, Prob11/505, fols 260–1v. Her daughter was alive in 1671: LMA, DW/PC/5/1670, 56. Stuchbury's name is sometimes given as Tutchbury, but this is incorrect.

CHAPTER 5

1. Richard Reynolds, *On Guerrilla Gardening* (London: Bloomsbury, 2008), p. 36; www.youtube.com: 'GGTV4: Red tulips at the Kremlin'.

2. Jake Halpern, 'The freegan establishment', *New York Times Magazine*, 4 June 2010; Tim Webb, 'Squatters', *N16 Magazine*, 25 (2005), 10; Andi Clevely, *The Allotment Book* (London: Collins, 2006), p. 11. See also Ashton Allotment Action statement at www.bobsbackyard.co.uk/AAA

3. Tony Benn, 'Land and freedom', *Guardian*, 1 May 1996.

4. Camilla Berens, 'Folk law: The New Diggers', *New Statesman & Society*, 5 May 1995; *Guardian*, 24 April 1995. Cf. George Monbiot, 'My hero: Gerrard Winstanley', *BBC History Magazine* (June 2000).

5. 'Levellers 350yr Anniversary' and 'Diggers Occupation April 1999' on www.youtube.com; 'Diggers 350' press releases on www.tlio.org.uk; messages on http://groups.yahoo.com/group/diggers350; *Guardian*, 24 March, 5 April 1999.

6. *Manchester Guardian*, 11 February 1908.

7. *Manchester Guardian*, 12 October, 8, 16 November 1905, 11, 14, 15, 16, 19, 20, 21, 23, 24, 25, 26 July, 6 August, 2, 4 September 1906, 6 February 1907.

8. *San Francisco Call*, 13 August 1906.

9. A. Stewart Gray, letter to the editor, *Manchester Guardian*, 23 July 1906.

10. *Manchester Guardian*, 17 February 1908.

11. *Manchester Guardian*, 6, 19, 27 February, 1, 20 March, 10 April, 29 May, 10, 11 December 1907, 8, 13 January 1908.

12. *Manchester Guardian*, 6, 10, 11, 12, 13, 14, 17, 21 February, *Observer*, 9 February 1908.

13. *Manchester Guardian*, 14 February 1908. Cf. *Manchester Courier and Lancashire General Advertiser*, 13 February 1908.

14. *The Times*, 17 August, 11, 12 September, 5, 13, 14 October; *Penny Illustrated Paper and Illustrated Times*, 22 August,

10 October; *Manchester Guardian*, 2, 5, 7 November 1908, 22 January, 11 February 1909.

15. *The Times*, 24, 29, 30 March, 20 April 1909; A. Stewart Gray, 'Art through the medium (one way out)', *The English Review*, February 1921, 167–72.

16. Obituary, *The Times*, 16 April 1937; Jacob Epstein, *Let there be Sculpture* (New York: G.P. Putnam's Sons, 1940), p. 102. John also knew of Winstanley: see his *Finishing Touches*, ed. D. George (London: Jonathan Cape Ltd, 1966), p. 147.

17. John Gurney, 'Gerrard Winstanley and the left' (forthcoming).

18. BL, Add. MS 37, 344, fols 283v-4; Bulstrode Whitelocke, *Memorials of the English Affairs* (1682), pp. 383–4.

19. Gurney, 'Winstanley and the left'.

20. Dennis Hardy, *Alternative Communities in Nineteenth-Century England* (London: Longman, 1979), pp. 181–3, 187–92, 199–207; Nigel Todd, *Roses and Revolutionists: The Story of the Clousden Hill Free Communist and Co-operative Colony* (London: People's Publications, 1986); Howkins, 'From Diggers to Dongas', 13–17.

21. Gurney, 'Winstanley and the left'.

22. Joseph Clayton, *Leaders of the People* (London: Martin Secker, 1910), p. 294.

23. Fenner Brockway, *Britain's First Socialists: The Levellers, Agitators and Diggers of the English Revolution* (London: Quartet Books, 1980). Cf. Brockway, *Towards Tomorrow: the Autobiography of Fenner Brockway* (London: Hart-Davis, MacGibbon, 1977), p. 20.

24. Tony Benn, *Against the Tide: Diaries 1973–1976* (London: Hutchinson, 1989), pp. 50, 54; Tony Benn, 'Leveller spirit', *Guardian*, 15 May 1976.

25. *The Times*, 3 May 1961.

26. Tony Benn, foreword to Brockway, *Britain's First Socialists*, ix–xi; Eric Heffer, foreword to Bernstein's *Cromwell and Communism* (reprint, Nottingham: Spokesman, 1980).

27. Needham wrote about Winstanley in his *Levellers in the English Revolution*, published under the name 'Henry Holorenshaw'.

28. A.L. Morton, *A People's History of England* (London: Gollancz, for the Left Book Club, 1938), p. 250.

29. Dell, 'Winstanley and the Diggers', esp. 138–9.

30. Hill and Dell, *Good Old Cause*, pp. 381–97.

31. Morton, *English Revolution*, p. 15. Cf. Morton, *People's History* (second edition, London: Lawrence & Wishart, 1948), pp. 259–60.

32. Cf. Bill Schwarz, '"The people" in history: The Communist Party Historians' Group, 1946–56', in Richard Johnson, Gregor McLennan, Bill Schwarz and David Sutton (eds.), *Making Histories: Studies in History-Writing and Politics* (London: Hutchinson, 1982), pp. 54–5, 71–4, 80.

33. Christopher Hill, 'Historians on the rise of British capitalism', *Science & Society*, XIV, 4 (Fall 1950), 321.

34. Hill and Dell, *Good Old Cause*, p. 401. Cf. Hill, *English Revolution 1640*, p. 68; Worden, *Roundhead Reputations*, p. 335.

35. Ibid., pp. 334–7; Ariel Hessayon, 'Fabricating radical traditions', *Cromohs Virtual Seminars*, 1–6.

36. G.F. Eckstein (C.L.R. James), 'Ancestors of the proletariat', *Fourth International*, 10, 8 (1949), 252–55 (accessed on www.marxists.org).

37. For Manning's politics see James Holstun, 'Brian Manning and the dialectics of revolt', *International Socialism*, 103 (2004); David Renton, 'Brian Manning (1927–2004)', *Revolutionary History*, 9, 1 (2005), 238–41; David Renton and Keith Flett, 'Brian Manning: radical historian of the English revolution', *Guardian*, 26 June 2004.

38. Manning, *Far Left*, p. 17. Cf. Manning, *1649*, p. 157.

39. Brian Manning, 'The peasantry and the English revolution', *Journal of Peasant Studies*, 2, 2 (1975), 133–58; Manning, review of Bradstock, *Winstanley and the Diggers*, 229–38. Cf. Carlin, *First English Revolution*, pp. 22, 29, 40, 41.

40. George Woodcock, *Anarchism: A History of Libertarian Ideas and Movement* (Cleveland: Meridian Books, 1962), p. 49.

41. Jeff Kisseloff, *Generation on Fire: Voices of Protest from the 1960s* (Lexington: University Press of Kentucky, 2007), p. 145; Timothy Miller, *The 60s Communes: Hippies and Beyond* (New York: Syracuse University Press, 1999), p. 3. The choice of Digger name is credited to 'another member of the troupe' in Emmett Grogan, *Ringolevio: A Life Played for Keeps* (New York: New York Review Books, 1990), p. 237.

42. Fred Davis, 'Why all of us may be hippies some day', in Donald L. Michael (ed.), *The Future Society* (Chicago: Aldine Publishing Co., 1970), p. 58; Miller, *Communes*, p. 45; Bryan D. Palmer,

Canada's 1960s: The Ironies of Identity in a Rebellious Era (Toronto: University of Toronto Press, 2009), pp. 204–7. See also the collection of 'Digger archives' at www.diggers.org

43. *International Times* (*IT*), 8 (13–26 February 1967), p. 11 (article reprinted from the *San Francisco Chronicle*). Cf. Elizabeth Nelson, *The British Counter-Culture, 1966–73* (London: Macmillan, 1989), pp. 74–7.

44. Kenneth Leech, *Youthquake* (London: Sheldon Press, 1973), pp. 41, 138; Clem Gorman, *People Together* (London: Paladin, 1975), p. 46.

45. Kevin Brownlow, *Winstanley: Warts and All* (London: UKA Press, 2009), p. 165.

46. 'Tribal stirrings', *IT*, 31 (17–30 May 1968). Cf. *IT*, 28 (5–18 April 1968).

47. *IT*, 28 (5–18 April), 31 (17–30 May 1968); *Guardian*, 13 April, 2 May 1968, 27 September 1969; Leech, *Youthquake*, p. 138.

48. *Oz*, 36 (July 1971), 25; Gorman, *People Together*, pp. 46, 111.

49. Crispin Aubrey and John Shearlaw, *Glastonbury: An Oral History of the Music, Mud and Magic* (London: Ebury Press, 2005), p. 26.

50. *Observer*, 4 March 1973; Brownlow, *Winstanley*, pp. 187, 201–3; Rawle obituaries: *Guardian*, 15 September; *Daily Telegraph*, 9 September 2010.

51. People was the name first given to the movement which in 1975 became the Ecology Party and from 1985 the Green Party.

52. The Central Library, Cambridge (CCL), Cambridgeshire Collection: C33.3 (election material, February 1974).

53. CCL, C33.3; *The Times*, 22 February 1974; CCL, election press cuttings: *Cambridge Evening News* (*CEN*), 18, 19, 20, 25, 27 February 1974.

54. CCL, cuttings: *CEN*, 1 March 1974.

55. CCL, cuttings: *CEN*, 19 November 1975.

56. 'Eddies: digging for victory', *Undercurrents*, 6 (March–April 1974).

57. Martyn Partridge, 'Rise up, ye noble Diggers', *Undercurrents*, 13 (November–December 1975), 24; *Girton College Annual Review, 2011*, pp. 137–8.

58. Ecology Party, *Politics for Life* (London: the Ecology Party, 1983), p. 24.

59. On Winstanley and the green movement see esp. Ariel Hessayon, 'Restoring the Garden of Eden in England's green and pleasant

land: The Diggers and the fruits of the earth', *Journal for the Study of Radicalism*, 2 (2008), 1–25.

60. Hill, *World Turned Upside Down*, pp. 236–7. Cf. Hessayon, 'Fabricating radical traditions'.

61. Hill, *World Turned Upside Down*, pp. 236–7, 245, 275; Hill, *Law of Freedom*, pp. 66–8.

62. David Caute, *Comrade Jacob* (London: A. Deutsch, 1961); David Caute, 'Looking back in regret at Winstanley', *Guardian*, 17 October 2008. For earlier literary references to the Diggers see Gurney, 'Winstanley and the left'.

63. *The Times*, 18 September 1962; *Guardian*, 28 November 1969.

64. Brownlow, *Winstanley*, pp. 69–70, 235; Caute, 'Looking back'. Caute also felt that the question of Winstanley's hold over his followers was not adequately addressed. Cf. John C. Tibbetts, '*Winstanley*: or, Kevin Brownlow camps out on St George's Hill', *Literature/Film Quarterly*, 31: 4 (2003).

65. Brownlow, *Winstanley*, pp. 51–2, 54, 71–5, 85, 178–9, 188–90.

66. Ibid., pp. 267–72, 297–303; Kevin Brownlow, 'It didn't happen here', *New Statesman*, 3 August 1979. Cf. William Egerton (ed.), *Memoirs of Peasant Tolstoyans in Soviet Russia* (Bloomington: Indiana University Press, 1993), xvi–xvii.

67. Caryl Churchill, *Light Shining in Buckinghamshire* (London: Pluto Press, 1978); Keith Dewhurst, *The World Turned Upside Down*, in his *War Plays* (London: Oberon, 1996).

68. Chris Stagg and Paul Hodson, *The World Turned Upside Down* (Brighton Actors' Workshop: Nightingale Theatre, Brighton, 1985; Tron, Glasgow, 1987).

69. *Light Shining* theatre programme: Royal National Theatre mobile production (1996–7; Cottesloe, 1997). Cf. *Guardian*, 11 January 1997.

70. Caryl Churchill, *Plays One* (London: Methuen, 1985), p. 183. The Digger connections were less explicit in the 2010 revival at the Arcola Theatre, London.

71. On camps see esp. Brian Doherty, 'Manufactured vulnerability: protest camp tactics', in Benjamin Seel, Matthew Paterson and Brian Doherty (eds.), *Direct Action in British Environmentalism* (London: Routledge, 2000), pp. 62–78.

72. Leon Rosselson, 'The World Turned Upside Down (Part Two – Song of the Diggers)', in Leon Rosselson and Jeff Parks, *For the Good of the Nation* (London: Journeyman Press, 1981), p. 64.

73. Leon Rosselson, *That's Not the Way It's Got to Be* (LP, Acorn Records, 1975); Dick Gaughan, *Handful of Earth* (LP, Topic Records, 1989); Billy Bragg, *Between the Wars* (EP, Go! Discs, 1985); Tony Benn and Roy Bailey, *The Writing on the Wall* (CD, Fuse, 2003).

74. Ian Sinclair, 'Leon Rosselson interview', *Morning Star*, 16 August 2007; Taylor, 'Rosselson interview'; Leon Rosselson, *The World Turned Upside Down: Rosselsongs 1960–2010* (CD, Fuse Records/PM Press, 2011), notes, p. 31; 'Our Diggers' song', *Greenham Common Women's Peace Camp Songbook*, song no. 24, at www.fredsakademiet.dk/abase/sange/greenham/song24.htm

75. Taylor, 'Rosselson interview'; Bradstock, *Winstanley and the Diggers*, p. 2; Rosselson at Occupy London on www.youtube.com; http://wellsocialists.org.uk/diggersfestival2012.asp

76. E.P. Thompson, *The Making of the English Working Class* (Harmondsworth: Pelican Books, 1968), pp. 210, 508, 659, 691, 703; Worden, *Roundhead Reputations*, pp. 206, 231; A. Temple Patterson, *Radical Leicester* (Leicester: University College, 1954), p. 318.

77. Clifford Harper, *Anarchists: Portraits* (London: Freedom Press, 1994); Clifford Harper, with Colin Ward, *Designs for Anarchist Postage Stamps* (London: Rebel Press, 1997); Oscar Zarate, *Winstanley* film poster, for The Other Cinema (1975).

78. *Graphic*, 12 August 1876; *The Times*, 8 January 1912.

79. *The Times*, 8 January 1912, 28 June 1913; *Observer*, 10 March, 13 October 1912; *St George's Hill and the Diggers* (Elmbridge Museum, exhibition booklet, 1999), pp. 12–15.

80. See for instance Iain Sinclair, *London Orbital* (London: Penguin Books, 2003), pp. 302, 305, 307–9.

81. http://telegraph.co.uk (27 May) and readers' comments; www.dailymail.co.uk (28 May 2011) and comments. Cf. http://ianbone.wordpress.com

82. Rosselson and Parks, *For the Good of the Nation*, p. 64.

Index